Serialization in Literature Across Media and Markets

Serialization is an old narrative strategy and a form of publication that can be traced far back in literary history, yet serial narratives are as popular as ever. This book investigates a resurgence of serial narratives in contemporary literary culture.

Analyzing series as diverse as Mark Z. Danielewski's experimental book series *The Familiar*, audiobook series by the Swedish streaming service Storytel, children's books by Lemony Snicket and Philip Pullman and their adaptations into screen, and serial writing and reading on the writing site Wattpad, the book traces how contemporary series at once are shaped by literary tradition and develop the format according to the logics of new media and digital technologies.

The book sheds light on the interplay between the selected serials' narrative content and medial, social, and economic contexts, drawing on insights from literary studies, literary sociology, media studies, and cultural studies. *Serialization in Literature Across Media and Markets* thus contributes a unique and interdisciplinary perspective on a historical phenomenon that has proved ever more successful in contemporary media culture.

Sara Tanderup Linkis (born in 1986), PhD in Comparative Literature, is a postdoc at Lund University, Sweden. Her research on serial narratives, transmediality, audiobooks, and multimodal literature is published in international journals as *Narrative, Orbis Litterarum*, and *Paradoxa*. She is the author of the monograph *Memory, Intermediality, and Literature* (Routledge, 2019).

Serialization in Literature Across Media and Markets

Sara Tanderup Linkis

NEW YORK AND LONDON

First published 2022
by Routledge
605 Third Avenue, New York, NY 10158

and by Routledge
2 Park Square, Milton Park, Abingdon, Oxon, OX14 4RN

Routledge is an imprint of the Taylor & Francis Group, an informa business

© 2022 Sara Tanderup Linkis

The right of Sara Tanderup Linkis to be identified as author of this work has been asserted in accordance with sections 77 and 78 of the Copyright, Designs and Patents Act 1988.

All rights reserved. No part of this book may be reprinted or reproduced or utilised in any form or by any electronic, mechanical, or other means, now known or hereafter invented, including photocopying and recording, or in any information storage or retrieval system, without permission in writing from the publishers.

Trademark notice: Product or corporate names may be trademarks or registered trademarks, and are used only for identification and explanation without intent to infringe.

Library of Congress Cataloging-in-Publication Data
A catalog record for this book has been requested

ISBN: 978-0-367-60809-5 (hbk)
ISBN: 978-1-032-20914-2 (pbk)
ISBN: 978-1-003-26589-4 (ebk)

DOI: 10.4324/9781003265894

Typeset in Times New Roman
by Apex CoVantage, LLC

For Jonathan, Pelle, and Ronja.

Contents

Acknowledgments viii

1 Introduction 1

2 "A different kind of pace." Bookish Seriality in Mark Z. Danielewski's *The Familiar* 15

3 "The End is really the middle of the story." Transmedial Seriality in Lemony Snicket's *A Series of Unfortunate Events* 34

4 Across Worlds and Volumes. Serial Space in Philip Pullman's *His Dark Materials* 52

5 Keep listening! Born-Audio Serials and Serialization as a Business Model 69

6 "Ilysm!" Serial Writing and Social Reading on Wattpad 86

7 Conclusion 103

Bibliography 113
Index 121

Acknowledgments

This book is a product of the research project, "Serialization in Contemporary Literary Culture," funded by the Independent Research Fund Denmark and conducted by me at Lund University in 2018–2020. It is also a product of multiple fruitful collaborations, some of which preceded this project, while others developed as a result of it.

I first and foremost owe thanks to my former supervisor and colleague at Aarhus University, Tore Rye Andersen, who shares my interest in serial narratives and who originally initiated a larger research project focusing on this issue. We never received funding for that collaborative project, but this book would not have been the same without Tore's ideas, feedback, and support. Furthermore, I want to thank colleagues at the Center for Literature between Media at Aarhus University for their interest and valuable comments and feedback over the years. The book was also developed in collaboration with my new colleagues at Lund University. Like my research in general, it has benefitted significantly from the unique interdisciplinary environment at the Department of Cultural Sciences at Lund University, where I have been able to combine perspectives from my background in literary studies with ideas and perspectives from publishing studies and studies in digital cultures. I furthermore owe thanks to Julia Pennlert, University of Borås for fruitful collaboration, which has resulted in work that also informs this book. I am grateful to Søren Vestergaard Poulsen, head of content and publishing at Storytel's subsidiary in Denmark, Mofibo, who has helped me greatly with conversations on the streaming service's use of the serial format.

Most of the book was written in 2020–2021, during the Covid-19 pandemic, and the writing process was prolonged because of the new reality with homeschooling children and online teaching. I want to give my deepfelt thanks to my editor at Routledge, Jennifer Abbott, for her understanding and patience in this situation. She and her team have been a great support during the whole process, from my initial proposal to the final book.

Finally, I want to thank my family. The fact that most of the actual writing of the book took place at home because of the pandemic has proved both challenging and rewarding. My children, Jonathan, Pelle, and Ronja, have endured exposure to several series in television, film, book, and audiobook formats. I hope some of this exposure, at least, will prove beneficial in the long run and that my children will be as enchanted by these series as I am, even if I may also be accused of being an old-fashioned mom who insists that we should read the books before watching the show.

1 Introduction

In 2015, the novel *One Rainy Day in May* by Mark Z. Danielewski was published. The novel in itself was remarkable: monumental 880 pages of experimental storytelling in text and images, multiple plotlines, typographic experiments, and text in various languages. However, the most remarkable thing about *One Rainy Day in May* was the fact that it was the first installment in a book series, *The Familiar*, which was planned to be developed in 27 volumes, reflecting the ambition of producing the literary equivalent of a modern television series. In 2016, the Swedish subscription service for audiobooks and e-books, Storytel, launched their new brand of serial audiobooks, Storytel Originals.[1] Storytel Originals are popular genre fiction, written specifically for the audiobook format and organized in episodes and seasons. At first glance, these popular stories do not have anything in common with Danielewski's experimental book series—except for the serial format. Both cases reflect what may be described as a resurgence of serialization in contemporary literary culture, a situation where literary producers, authors, and publishers increasingly turn toward serial narratives and modes of publication and distribution.

This book aims to investigate this resurgence of serialization in literary culture and across media. Serial narratives are nothing new; the format may be traced back to 19th-century feuilleton novels and have been continuously present ever since within various genres and media. However, recent years have seen a renewed interest in serialization as an esthetic strategy, a cultural practice, and a business model within all forms of cultural production. This development may be connected to ongoing transformations in how literature is produced, distributed, and consumed. This book sheds new light on these developments by focusing on serial literary works, and worlds, and serial consumers and producers. Selected cases include specific works, such as Danielewski's *The Familiar*, the children's book series *A Series of Unfortunate Events* by Lemony Snicket, and *His Dark Materials* by Philip Pullman, as well as Storytel's Originals brand and serial publication and

DOI: 10.4324/9781003265894-1

consumption on the writing site Wattpad. Focusing on these cases, the book investigates how literary culture in the 21st century is influenced by the logics of other serial media and digital culture at various levels: both when it comes to changes in the narrative organization and esthetic content of serial texts and when it comes to modes of producing, distributing, and consuming serial narratives.

The book's emphasis on literature serves to limit the perspective, while the focus on serialization as a transmedial practice also contributes to highlighting the ongoing integration of literary culture into contemporary media culture. Thus, the book does not approach literature as an isolated field of study but rather focuses on the relation between the textual content of serial texts and the medial, social, and economic contexts. In this way, I contribute to the development of new interdisciplinary perspectives on serialization, drawing on existing research in serials and serial culture informed by narratology, media studies, cultural studies, and literary history and highlighting the connections between these perspectives. I investigate how contemporary literary culture at once returns to the serial forms of narrative and modes of publication that characterize the Victorian age and transforms these forms according to the logics of digital media and modern popular culture. Accordingly, the book not only sheds light on serial literature and transformations in literary culture but also offers perspectives on serialization as a broader phenomenon, a widespread transmedial practice rooted in literary history while reflecting the changing modes of producing, distributing, and consuming narratives enabled by digitalization and new media.

From Dickens to Storytel: The Literary History of Serialization

By *serialization*, I mean the production and publication of narratives in smaller parts or installments. The concept of serialization is related but not identical to *seriality*, which refers to a general principle: the non-hierarchical and successive organization of parts or numbers. The result is a *series*, or a *serial*: the latter usually understood to be more specific than the former, as the serial refers to an ongoing narrative organized in parts, while a series is merely a successive organization of parts.[2] As noted by Ruth Page, the concept of seriality is not necessarily associated with narrativity.[3] However, since I am primarily interested in developing new perspectives on serial literature, this book is first and foremost about serialization as a narrative strategy.

As a narrative strategy, serialization originates in literary culture. In the mid-17th century, publishers began to publish parts of narratives in pamphlets. This development was part of the broader democratization of print culture as pamphlets would be more affordable than bound books for many readers. Thus, from the beginning, serialization has been related to the popularization of literature and to commercial conditions as well as esthetic motifs, and the history of the format exemplifies how literary texts are shaped historically by economic and social contexts, in this case, by the economic conditions of the intended audience and by developments in book production.

In the 19th century, serialization became widespread, and in a literary context, it is often associated with Victorian feuilleton culture. Authors such as Charles Dickens, Alexandre Dumas, and Gustave Flaubert first published their popular works in feuilleton format, in literary journals or newspapers. Only later were these works collected into the monumental bound volumes, which we today commonly associate with 19th-century literature. Focusing on the original serial format of these works provides an opportunity for studying the works in relation to their original material and medial contexts, and much existing research in serialization within literary studies and book history consequently focuses on this period.[4]

In the 20th century, the publication of feuilleton novels was largely abandoned, as bound volumes became more affordable for most readers. Serialization became primarily associated with new forms of popular culture and emerging mass media, such as radio and television.[5] The connection between seriality and mass media has been discussed by, among others, Roger Hagedorn, who points out that new mass media have historically employed serial narratives in order to "develop the commercial exploitation"[6] of that specific medium. He notes,

> By tracing the history of the serial, we can recognize that as new media technology is introduced commercial exploiters have consistently turned to the serial form of narrative presentation precisely in order to cultivate a dependable audience of consumers. This audience is then available and predisposed to consume other types of texts provided by the medium in question. In this way, individual serials function not only to increase newspaper circulation, the sale of theatre tickets, or increasingly expensive advertising spots, but more significantly they serve to *promote the medium in which they appear*.[7]

To demonstrate this idea, Hagedorn traces the history of serialization from print culture to radio feuilletons, comics, and television series, and he argues that, in each of these cases, series are used to promote the medium in question and make it widely popular. Once the medium has been established as a mass medium, the serial format gives way to other formats such as bound books.

It is certainly possible to question Hagedorn's linear account of the history of seriality. According to Hagedorn, once a new medium turns into a mass medium, the serial format is usually abandoned within that medium and displaced by other forms of narrative presentation. Accordingly, he states, "the serial has been . . . a consistent loser."[8] However, serial narratives often continue to occur within those media where the format is no longer predominant. Serial literature, for instance, never disappeared but has been consistently present in literary history, and during the 20th century, it was primarily associated with genre fiction, such as romance and crime fiction. Furthermore, as this book will demonstrate, it is possible to point to a resurgence of the serial format within older media or art forms, such as literature, as these are influenced by new media and technologies. Hagedorn is, however, right in emphasizing the historical connection between seriality and popular culture. Frank Kelleter also highlights this aspect, emphasizing how serialized narratives since early newspaper novels in the 19th century are historically associated with a process of popularization, expanding the reading public and reaching new groups of consumers.[9]

Following Kelleter and Hagedorn, it is tempting to consider serialization as a practice in popular culture that is primarily connected with the commercial exploitation of mass media. However, it should be noted that the history of seriality reaches beyond popular culture, as several established authors from Gustave Flaubert to James Joyce and Thomas Pynchon also initially published their works, or parts of their works, in serial format.[10] This fact has more or less been forgotten in literary criticism because 20th-century textual scholarship has emphasized the idea of the literary work as a finite and autonomous entity. There has not been much interest within literary studies in the material aspects or the production processes and publication contexts surrounding literary works. However, recent efforts within media-oriented literary analyses and book history, as represented by, for example, N. Katherine Hayles and Jerome McGann, pave the way for including such aspects in literary analysis.[11] Both Hayles and McGann argue for a new emphasis on literary texts' medial and material conditions, drawing on insights from related disciplines such as book history, media studies, and publishing studies. Notably, this new awareness within literary studies of the material conditions of literature may be linked to the process of digitalization: as literature migrates into other formats and media, the printed book can no longer be taken for granted, and it becomes relevant to consider alternative literary formats, even in a historical perspective.

The new interest in seriality and serial narratives, exemplified by this book, may thus have as much to do with the increasing awareness of the significance of the medial and material contexts of literature in the digital age as it has to do with actual changes in the way literature is produced, distributed, and consumed. Yet, I argue, such changes also take place in contemporary literary culture. Although it is possible to trace a continuous history of serialization, recent years have seen an increasing dominance of serial productions. This development may be considered, among other things, as a result of the process of digitalization. The book investigates how serial forms of narrative and modes of publication are currently revived and developed as a consequence of the new conditions for the production, distribution, and reception of literature that new media and technologies bring along. The spread of e-books and audiobooks, for instance, paves the way for releasing novels in installments that can be published continually and accessed immediately online. Storytel's focus on the serial format with their Originals series may be considered in this context, as may the different types of serial narratives that are published via social media and digital platforms: Jennifer Egan, for instance, published her short story "Black Box" (2015) on Twitter, in a series of tweets,[12] Margaret Atwood published her novel *Positron* (2013) serially with the online publisher Byliner, and Julian Fellowes first published his bestselling *Belgravia* series in digitalized serial format, with weekly releases of the 11 installments to be downloaded with an app.[13]

Notably, these digital distribution methods also lead away from the logics of mass media that Hagedorn and Kelleter emphasize and toward more individualized modes of serial consumption. We no longer have to read, watch, or listen to the same stories at the same time through the same (mass) media because it is possible to watch on-demand, binge-watch series on Netflix or listen to serialized audiobooks via Storytel while jogging or doing housework. Thus, digitalization has changed serial production, distribution, and consumption conditions, challenging the established connections between seriality, popular culture, and mass media.

Serialization, however, not only gains currency in digital publication contexts, but the contemporary book market is also dominated by book series: We may think of such diverse titles as Karl Ove Knausgaard's autobiographical series *My Struggle*, Elena Ferrante's Neapolitan-novels, George R.R. Martin's *A Song of Ice and Fire*, or the two children's book series analyzed in this book: Snicket's *A Series of Unfortunate Events* and Pullman's *His Dark Materials*. These are all bestselling titles, reflecting Ann Steiner's observation that serialization is one of the features that make a bestseller in 21st-century book culture.[14] According to Steiner, this is "due to publishers pushing for series as it is easier to retain interest in a book when there is a sequel, but it is also due to many readers looking for long narratives that promise a continued story."[15] Notably, while originating in print format, many of the titles mentioned earlier are also known for their serial adaptation in television or film series, which furthermore, according to Steiner, strengthens their position as bestsellers.[16] In many cases, the process of serialization is connected to processes of adaptation, and as several of my analyses demonstrate, some adaptations may even present a further narrative development of the series in question. Margaret Atwood's *The Handmaid's Tale* (1985) is an interesting recent example of this tendency. Initially, a non-serial novel, *The Handmaid's Tale* was turned into a television series by HBO in 2017. The television series developed the story beyond the original book's plot, and this new development became the foundation for Atwood's new novel, *Testaments* (2019), which presents a continuation of events that were first presented in the television series. Thus, via the adaptation, the original novel was turned into a book series.

In this way, the revived interest in serial narratives spans different genres and media. The concept of transmediality and transmedia storytelling, as developed by Henry Jenkins, becomes significant here. In *Convergence Culture*, Jenkins describes how narratives are increasingly developed across media in a culture dominated by the logics of media convergence.[17] While the present book focuses on serialization in literary culture, it is based on an idea of literature as an art form that moves between media, beyond the printed book. Furthermore, as addressed by Jenkins, media audiences also increasingly move across platforms, and this tendency also applies to readers, accessing literary texts in different formats and via different platforms such as Storytel or Wattpad, discussed in this book. Literary culture is thus affected by the overall logics of modern media culture. Accordingly, the book reflects the assumption that serialized literature should be studied not in isolation but in relation to a broader cultural development where serialization has become widespread to the extent that it has been called the dominant logic of modern culture.[18]

This development is most evidently reflected in the fact that modern television series have entered a golden age. The so-called quality television series such as *The Wire, Sopranos, Breaking Bad*, and *The Handmaid's Tale* receive critical acclaim and are presented as the "great novels" of our time.[19] The logic of serialization also dominates the movie, video game, and comics industries. It especially becomes central with the increasing dominance of streaming in modern cultural industries, where subscription-based streaming services such as Netflix or Storytel use the format to maintain consumers' loyalty to a platform, making users keep paying their subscription, month after month, in order to have access to ongoing series, episode after episode.[20] Serialization, in this context, appears not merely as a form of narrative organization but also as a business model.

Investigating the resurgence of serialized literature in relation to this broader development, this book sheds light on serialization as a widespread cultural practice, reflecting and affecting how we produce and consume narratives in modern culture. Thus, I ask, what is the esthetic and narrative as well as commercial power of serial narratives? Why do they re-emerge now, and how are they circulated and developed according to the logics of modern media culture?

Stories, Media, and Markets

To answer these questions, the book draws on the existing research on serialization, which is, as mentioned, rooted in different disciplines. Significant contributions originate within media studies and cultural studies focusing on serialization in modern mass media, especially television and film. Frank Kelleter's anthology *Media of Serial Narratives* (2017) and Rob Allen and Thijs van den Berg's *Serialization in Popular Culture* (2014) exemplify the strong tendency within this tradition to emphasize the connection between seriality and popular culture.[21] Research originating within literary studies, on the other hand, often focuses on a historical perspective, on Victorian feuilleton novels, just as research efforts within periodical studies and book history tend to concentrate on serial publishing in the 19th century.[22] A significant foundation for understanding individual serialized works and phenomena has thus been established, but the field of seriality studies has also been characterized by a relatively segmented approach, as most studies focus on either text-centered approaches or media-oriented analyses and either 19th-century literature or modern mass media. However, recent years have seen the emergence of interdisciplinary perspectives on serialization, highlighting especially the significance of transmedial dynamics and the impact of digital media and formats on serial narratives and culture.[23]

This book should be considered in relation to this latter tendency, presenting, for the first time, a systematic study of serialization in contemporary literary culture. Through an interdisciplinary approach, drawing on perspectives from the different disciplines outlined earlier, I investigate how contemporary serialized works rely on literary tradition while also developing the format according to new media conditions and to the logics of serial popular culture. To capture how selected works and actors navigate between embracing literary tradition and adjusting to modern media culture, the book thus combines a text-centered approach, focusing on narrative and esthetic aspects, with a media-oriented approach and with an approach informed by cultural studies and literary sociology, focusing on the social and economic aspects of serialization.

A Text-Centered Approach: Narrative Aspects

The series as a form of narrative is characterized by certain recurrent narrative features: It often employs cutting-off techniques and cliff-hangers in order to create suspense and maintain interest; it dilutes the idea of the ending and typically balances between repetition and variation.[24] Drawing on established narrative theories on seriality and serialization, I examine how these narrative features are still used effectively today in, for instance, Storytel's audiobook feuilletons and serial writing on Wattpad. Yet, I also argue that, despite these recurrent features, the serial narrative form has not stayed the same. The book accordingly traces how the narrative content of literary series is transformed in contemporary literature and culture, drawing new theoretical work on series and seriality by, for example, Jason Mittell and Marie-Laure Ryan. Mittell, who focuses on the contemporary developments in modern television series, challenges Umberto Eco's classic definition of seriality, which emphasizes the aspect of repetition. "To serialize means to repeat,"[25] according to Eco, but according to Mittell, contemporary series are characterized by variation rather than repetition and increasing narrative complexity.[26] While Mittell argues that this development is specific for television series, I demonstrate how it may also be observed in relation to the literary series by, for example, Mark Z. Danielewski and Lemony Snicket. Furthermore, my analyses are informed by a recent tendency within narratology to move from focusing on "narratives" toward emphasizing the idea of narrative worlds or "storyworlds" as described by Marie-Laure Ryan,[27] and I explore the concept of the serial storyworld in Chapter 4, focusing on works by Philip Pullman. Thus, I am basically interested in exploring how the serial format is transformed by the way we tell stories and construct narrative worlds in contemporary culture.

A Media-Oriented Approach: Medial and Intermedial Aspects

Serialization was originally connected to 19th-century print culture but has since moved into other media. Thus, feedback loops between different media occur. For instance, while television series originally appeared to be inspired by the feuilleton format of Victorian novels, new literary works, including the book series by Danielewski or Storytel's audiobook series, imitate the narrative form and format of television series. They are, for instance, organized in "episodes" and "seasons." In other cases, serial stories are developed across media, as I explore in relation to the works by Snicket and Pullman. Thus, departing from Mittell's argument about narrative complexity presented earlier, I introduce the concept of *transmedia complexity*, suggesting how the narrative structure of a given series may be complicated as the series is developed across media.

Addressing this situation where serial narratives are widely adapted for different media, Jim Collins argues that the medium becomes less significant and gives way to a primary interest in the "story," no matter the medium; he suggests that serial narratives "are no longer medium-specific."[28] However, I demonstrate that, despite, or perhaps exactly because of, increasing media convergence and transmedial storytelling, serial stories are significantly shaped by the medium in question and by the surrounding media culture, audiences, and platforms. Drawing on existing research on serial popular culture by, for example, Mittell and Kelleter[29] and comparing the medial affordances of printed books, audiobooks, and television series, I investigate how these different media recirculate and develop the serial narrative form.

A Sociological Approach: Social and Economic Aspects

Serialization is often associated with social reading cultures. As noted by Jennifer Hayward and Henry Jenkins, the serial format promotes active audiences and participatory cultures since the intervals between installments allow consumers to engage in the continuous creation of the works.[30] This is nothing new: Already, Dickens's novels were surrounded by active reader communities, and in the 20th century, television and film series were surrounded by similar participatory fan cultures. Digital culture does, however, enforce this aspect, providing new possibilities and platforms for social reading and participation in ongoing serial narratives, as exemplified by the online fan cultures that surround serial works such as *Harry Potter, Game of Thrones,* or for that matter, Danielewski's *The Familiar,* as discussed in Chapter 2. This development is often celebrated as one step toward a more democratic culture where consumers have the power to interact and participate in cultural production, as emphasized by Jenkins, among others.[31] However, I complicate this idea by investigating the commercial incentives of serial publishing, adapting an approach informed by literary sociology and publishing studies.[32] Serialization is generally related to economic interests: By publishing narratives in installments and encouraging participation, it is possible to maintain users' attention and build a loyal customer base over time. While this commercial function has always been associated with serial narratives, the logics of digitalization, including new forms of distribution, further contribute to stressing this mechanism.[33] Accordingly, I address the economic and social incentives of serialization in digital culture by studying serial producers, such as Storytel, and serial reading communities on Wattpad.

While the existing research tends to consider these narrative, medial, social, and economic aspects of serialization separately, I investigate how they are connected. This approach necessitates an interdisciplinary approach that combines narratological theory with perspectives from media studies and cultural studies and sociological theories of reader cultures and the book market. A significant contribution of the book is to demonstrate how the combination of these approaches may shed new light on serialization as well as on wider areas of literary and cultural production and consumption.

Chapter by Chapter

This book combines analyses of selected works with analyses of the works' commercial and medial contexts to investigate the esthetic, medial, social, and commercial aspects of serialization. The selection of works spans different languages, genres, and media. While my emphasis is on literature in the sense of verbal narratives, the works and cases all relate to serialization as a transmedial cultural practice.

Beginning with a work-centered approach, Chapter 2 focuses on the aforementioned series by Danielewski, *The Familiar*. I investigate how this contemporary book series at once imitates and resists the serial logics of modern media culture: *The Familiar* relates to the logics of modern television series at several different levels, and yet, despite the similarities, it also positions itself in stark contrast to new media culture and emphasizes the "bookishness" of the literary series. Exploring this ambiguity, the chapter contributes new knowledge about what happens to printed novels in the golden age of television series. It argues that, even though other serial media may inspire printed novels, the medium of print still matters for the kind of story that is told, the esthetic and narrative effects, and the kind of serial engagement that the work produces.

The relation between literature and television series is further explored in Chapter 3, which presents an analysis of the serial development in the children's series *A Series of Unfortunate Events* by Lemony Snicket (alias Daniel Handler). The book series has been criticized for its repetitive structure; however, drawing on theories on seriality by Mittell and Kelleter, the chapter demonstrates how the series moves beyond repetition. Furthermore, I examine how the recent television adaptation by Netflix adds to the development of serial complexity, rather than merely repeating the plot in the books. By thus comparing the book series and the Netflix adaptation, I argue that the series exemplifies what I call transmedial serial complexity.

Chapter 4 continues to examine this aspect, focusing on Philip Pullman's *His Dark Materials* trilogy and related materials. Specifically, I focus on serial representations of space and place in Pullman's work and on the series itself as a space for the reader to traverse. Drawing on Marie Laure Ryan's concept of transmedial storyworlds, I examine the development of

Pullman's series as it is expanded across different works, including analyses of Pullman's other works. I finally include HBO's television adaptation of *His Dark Materials*, which provides an opportunity to study how the relation between the serial and spatial dynamics in *His Dark Materials* is re-interpreted when remediated. Thus, the chapter provides an investigation of how places and spaces in Pullman's work are transformed across worlds, volumes, and media.

I supplement the work-centered approach in Chapters 2–4 with a sociological approach in Chapters 5 and 6, allowing me to address serialization not only as a way of telling and selling stories but also as a dominant cultural practice in the sense formulated by Peggy Miller and Jaqueline Goodnow: "actions that are repeated, shared with others in a social group, and invested with normative expectations and with meanings or significances that go beyond the immediate goals of the action."[34] Serialization as a cultural practice is shaped by the motivations of cultural producers and consumers, and accordingly, Chapters 5 and 6 focus on the production and consumption of literary serials. This also means that, while Chapters 2–4 all, to some extent, focus on the relation between literature and television series, in Chapters 5 and 6, I move on to focus on the broader consequences of digitalization for serial publishing and consumption. Chapter 5 examines the case of Storytel's audiobook feuilletons, Storytel Originals, which exemplify how new digital formats pave the way for new forms of serial narratives and return to the logics and modes of publishing, which characterized 19th-century feuilletons. I examine how Storytel uses serialization as a commercial strategy and how the serial format affects the esthetic content of a selected Originals series, *Virus* by the Swedish author Daniel Åberg.

Finally, Chapter 6 further explores modes of serial reading as I investigate the serial and social reading on the social writing site Wattpad. Wattpad is a site for amateur and professional authors to share and develop their written work in serial format. The chapter specifically analyzes the social interaction represented in and surrounding two serial novels, Margaret Atwood and Naomi Alderman's the *Happy Sunrise Zombie Home* (2013) and Anna Todd's bestselling series, *After* (2014). While both of these were written specifically for publication on Wattpad, they exemplify different uses of the platform and the serial format by two already established authors and by an (eventually successful) amateur writer, respectively. By comparing these cases, I am thus able to examine how the serial format is used in different ways on the platform and how these different approaches result in different social dynamics and reader cultures.

The five chapters cover different narrative, medial, social, and economic aspects of serialization. Moreover, each chapter illustrates how these aspects are connected in different ways. In the conclusion, I summarize

Introduction

my results, and I consider how the cases, when read together, contribute to shed new light on serialization as a cultural practice rooted in literary culture yet developed across media. Thus, by combining an emphasis on work-centered analysis with sociological and medial perspectives, I hope to provide new insights into the development of narratives across volumes, media, and markets in 21st-century literature.

Notes

1. See Jeppe Bangsgaard, "Føljetonen vender tilbage til litteraturen," *Berlingske*, January 5, 2016, www.b.dk/kultur/foeljetonen-vender-tilbage-til-litteraturen; Carsten Andersen, "Dansk forlag vil tage tv-serien tilbage til litteraturens territorium," *Politiken*, October 27, 2016, https://politiken.dk/kultur/boger/art5595116/Dansk-forlag-vil-tage-tv-serien-tilbage-til-litteraturens-territorium; Carsten Andersen, "Nu skal danskerne høre specialdesignede romaner, som vi streamer Netflix-serier," *Politiken*, October 27, 2017, https://politiken.dk/kultur/boger/art6171344/Nu-skal-danskerne-høre-specialdesignede-romaner-som-vi-streamer-Netflix-serier.
2. For a discussion of the relation between serials and series, see Tudor Oltean, "Series and Seriality in Media Culture," *European Journal of Communication* 8 (1993): 5–31.
3. Ruth Page, "Seriality and Storytelling in Social Media," *Storyworlds* 5 (2013): 31–54. As an example of non-narrative serialization, Page mentions Wikipedia, where each entry is produced serially, by multiple users.
4. For recent studies of 19th-century serial literature, see, e.g., Robert L. Patten, "Dickens as Serial Author. A Case of Multiple Identities," in *Nineteenth Century Media and the Construction of Identities*, eds. Laurel Brake, Bill Bell and David Finkelstein (London: Palgrave Macmillan, 2000), 137–53; Mark W. Turner, "The Unruliness of Serials in the Nineteenth Century (and in the Digital Age)," in *Serialization in Popular Culture*, eds. Rob Allen and Thijs van den Berg (New York: Routledge, 2014), 11–31.
5. For studies of serial narratives in television and other popular media, see Frank Kelleter, ed., *Media of Serial Narratives* (Columbia: The Ohio State University Press, 2017); Frank Kelleter, *Serial Agencies. The Wire and its Readers* (Hants: Zero Books, 2013); Jason Mittell, *Complex TV. The Poetics of Contemporary Television Storytelling* (New York: New York University Press, 2015).
6. Roger Hagedorn, "Technology and Economic Exploitation: The Serial as a Form of Narrative Presentation," *Wide Angle* 10, no. 4 (1988): 5.
7. Ibid.
8. Ibid.
9. Kelleter, *Serial Narratives*, 13.
10. Flaubert's *Madame Bovary* was serialized in *La Revue de Paris* in 1856, Joyce's *Ulysses* was serialized in parts in *The Little Review* 1918–1920, and parts of Thomas Pynchon's *The Crying of Lot 49* were published in *Esquire* in 1965.
11. See N. Katherine Hayles, *Writing Machines* (Cambridge, MA: MIT Press, 2002); Jerome McGann, *The Textual Condition* (Princeton: Princeton University Press, 1991).

12. For an analysis and discussion of serialized Twitter fiction, including Egan's work, see Tore Rye Andersen, "Staggered Transmissions: Twitter and the Return of Serialized Literature," *Convergence* 23, no. 1 (2017): 34–48.
13. Notably, both Egan, Atwood, and Fellowes later published their works in the format of printed books, suggesting the continuing status of print publishing within literary culture. Even the most successful of Storytel's Originals have been published in print. A Swedish Originals author, Daniel Åberg, describes the difficulties of gaining recognition within literary culture with digital formats. Thus, while digital serialization may serve to draw attention to the work in question and allow it to make it to the bestselling lists, it does not (yet) attract much critical acclaim and literary prizes. See Daniel Åberg, "At skrive til øret. Betragtninger fra en Storytel Originals forfatter," *Passage* 83 (2020): 71–84.
14. Ann Steiner, "Serendipity, Promotion, and Literature," in *Hype. Bestsellers and Literary Culture,* eds. Jon Helgason, Sara Kärrholm and Ann Steiner (Lund: Nordic Academic Press, 2014), 45.
15. Ibid.
16. Ibid.
17. Henry Jenkins, *Convergence Culture. Where Old and New Media Collide* (New York and London: New York University Press, 2006).
18. Sabine Sielke, "'Joy in Repetition': The Significance of Seriality for Memory and (Re)Mediation," in *The Memory Effect: The Remediation of Memory in Literature and Film,* eds. Russell Kilbourn and Eleanor Ty (Waterloo: Wilfrid Laurier University Press, 2013), 37–50.
19. See Jakob Isak Nielsen. "Tv-serien som vor tids roman?" *Passage* 68 (2012): 83–100; Jim Collins, "The Use Values of Narrativity in Digital Cultures," *New Literary History* 44 (2013): 639–60.
20. For further discussion of serialization in relation to the increasing dominance of streaming on the book market, see Karl Berglund and Sara Tanderup Linkis, "Modelling Subscription-Based Streaming Services for Books," *Memoires du Livre/Studies in Book Culture* (forthcoming). See also Sara Tanderup Linkis and Julia Pennlert, "Episodic Listening," *Journal of Electronic Publishing* 3, no. 20 (2021), https://doi.org/10.3998/3336451.0023.102.
21. See Kelleter, *Serial Narratives*; Allen and van den Berg, *Serialization in Popular Culture*. Other significant contributions include Kelleter, *Serial Agencies*; Mittell, *Complex TV*; Oltean, "Series"; Jennifer Poole Hayward, *Consuming Pleasures: Active Audiences and Serial Fictions from Dickens to Soap Opera* (Lexington: University Press of Kentucky, 1997). For a good overview of serialization as a cultural practice in Danish, see Tore Rye Andersen, *Serier* (Aarhus: Aarhus University Press, 2019).
22. See, e.g., Patten, "Serial Author"; Turner, "Unruliness." For a periodical studies approach, see Sam Latham and Robert Scholes, "The Rise of Periodical Studies," *PMLA* 121, no. 2 (2006): 517–31.
23. See Page, "Social Media"; Collins, "Use Value"; Andersen, "Staggered Transmissions"; Tore Rye Andersen and Sara Tanderup Linkis, "As We Speak. Concurrent Narration and Participation in the Serial Narratives *Skam* and @I_Bombadil," *Narrative* 27, no. 1 (2019): 83–106; Tanderup Linkis and Pennlert, "Episodic Listening."
24. See Frank Kermode, *The Sense of an Ending* (Oxford: Oxford University Press, 1967); Umberto Eco, *The Limits of Interpretation* (Bloomington and Indianapolis: Indiana University Press, 1991).

25. Eco, *Limits*, 85.
26. Mittell, *Complex TV*.
27. Marie-Laure Ryan and Jan-Noël Thon, eds., *Storyworlds Across Media* (Lincoln and London: University of Nebraska Press, 2014).
28. Collins, "Use Values," 653.
29. Mittell, *Complex TV*; Kelleter, *Serial Narratives*.
30. Hayward, *Consuming Pleasures*; Jenkins, *Convergence Culture*. For further perspectives on serial fandoms, see Anne Moore, "After the Break. Serial Narratives and Fannish Reading" (Diss., Tufts University, 2012).
31. Jenkins, *Convergence Culture*.
32. See, for instance, Claire Squires, *Marketing Literature* (London: Palgrave Macmillan, 2009); John B. Thompson, *Merchants of Culture* (London: Penguin, 2012); John B. Thompson, *Book Wars. The Digital Revolution in Publishing* (Cambridge: Polity Press, 2021).
33. For discussion of digital distribution on the commercial use of serials, see, e.g., Berglund and Tanderup Linkis, "Modelling." See also Padmini Ray Murray and Claire Squires, "The Digital Publishing Communications Circuit," *Book 2.0* 3, no. 1 (2013): 3–24.
34. Peggy J. Miller and Jaqueline Goodnow, "Cultural Practices: Toward an Integration of Culture and Development," *New Directions for Child Development* 67 (1995): 7.

2 "A different kind of pace." Bookish Seriality in Mark Z. Danielewski's *The Familiar*[1]

The fifth volume in Mark Z. Danielewski's book series *The Familiar* (2014–) was published on October 31, 2017. The novel *Redwood* was presented as the last volume in "season one" of the series and thus attained the status of a "season finale." The release accordingly led to much activity in the Facebook group devoted to the series, "The Familiar (volumes 1–5) Reading Club." Readers posted images of their new copies of the book and discussed the look, feel, physical quality, and smell (!) of the new book before any of them had had a chance to read it. Danielewski participated in the celebration by posting notifications for his tour around the United States and communicated with his fans through a Facebook live session. During the following weeks, the Facebook group developed into a space for analytical discussions of the book. The readers helped each other translate the many passages in foreign languages into English, and compared the text with other works: especially other series, such as Karl Ove Knausgaard's *My Struggle*, which Danielewski was reading at the time of publication, and the television series *Stranger Things*, the second season of which had just been released on Netflix, and which many readers were watching while reading the new *Familiar* volume.

The case of *The Familiar* thus relates to the transmedial aspect of contemporary serial culture, presented in my introduction. In this chapter, I read the series accordingly, as an example of how serial literature today is inspired by and incorporates the logics of other media and media cultures. As noted by Alison Gibbons, Danielewski's whole oeuvre can be considered a remediation project, each work focusing on a different medium and translating it into print.[2] *The Familiar*, which was planned to be developed in 27 volumes, specifically invokes the logics of modern television series. Danielewski reflects on this connection in an interview, noting how,

> Television series began to play a role. . . . You and I watched this cultural presence emerge and become pervasive. People were saying, "We are watching novels for the first time in way that film could never do."

DOI: 10.4324/9781003265894-2

> Then you have examples like *The Wire* where the pacing was about character. It wasn't about tearing up stories. It wasn't about creating an entire story in just one episode, which was the old mode for serial books. . . . Then *The Wire* came along and showed a different kind of pace. There was a combination of an appreciation for a series like *The Wire* or *The Sopranos*, or *Battlestar Galactica*. It influenced my view on how this whole thing would unfold.[3]

The Familiar is thus framed as a reaction to the "cultural presence" of television series in recent years. Jason Mittell and Jim Collins, among others, point out how television series have been culturally re-evaluated, especially since 2000: From being primarily associated with mainstream entertainment, the format has gained cultural status.[4] Mittell links this development to a turn in modern television storytelling toward more complex, continuing serial narratives.[5] Danielewski also reflects on this tendency, commenting on the "pacing" in *The Wire*, which is moving away from traditional episodic series, "an entire story in just one episode," and toward "a different kind of pace." It is this pacing, the pace of the continuing long-form serial narrative, that Danielewski wants to translate into print with his 27-volume project. Notably, while Mittell insists that the turn toward serial complexity is specific for television series, the development has often been described as television's turn toward the literary. Danielewski's comment that people are watching "novels" thus evokes the widespread discourse of referring to "quality" series such as *The Wire, The Sopranos*, and *Breaking Bad* as the "new novels."[6] How does serial literature react to this situation, where television series turn literary? Investigating how *The Familiar* imitates and remediates modern television series will allow me to examine how literature is affected by the logics of other serial media and media cultures.

The Familiar, does, however, present itself first and foremost as a book series. Like Danielewski's other works, it combines the remediation project with an exploration of the affordances of the printed book, exposing the visual and material qualities of the book as an object through experiments with typography and layout and through its sheer physical monumentality. I explore how the work thus transforms the serial format that we know from television by performing a bookish seriality. The chapter in this way sheds light on the serial format as it develops between media. I argue that, even though literary serials may be influenced by the narrative, social, and commercial logics of television series, and vice versa, the medium still matters for the kind of story that is told, for the narrative effects of seriality, and for the kind of serial engagement that the work produces.

Reinventing Television Series

The serial form of publication is well known to Danielewski. His breakthrough, the bestselling experimental novel *House of Leaves*, was first released as a feuilleton via the webpage iUniverse.com immediately before the printed book was published in 1999. Back then, the publishers Pantheon and iUniverse.com commented that serializing the work made it possible "to reinvent the historic Dickensian publishing formula—serialization of an entire work prior to publication—using a new technology."[7] However, while *House of Leaves* was only serialized as a form of online promotion of the already finished, printed novel, *The Familiar* was planned as a project that directly exhibits and reflects on the process of serialization. The work was, as mentioned, originally planned to be developed in 27 volumes, five of which have been published between 2014 and 2017. Together, these five volumes make up "season one"—reflecting the novel's inspiration from the terminology and structure of television series. While the series was eventually "paused" in 2018 due to declining sales, the serial ambition still dominates the presentation and framing of the work. Every volume is marked as a part of a series since each book's number in the series is presented with a large number on the front cover. Above the number appears the title of the series, *The Familiar*, in large letters, while the individual title of each volume, for instance, *Redwood* for volume five, appears in smaller letters. Thus, the books are first and foremost presented as parts of a bigger whole.

Opening the books, the reader is confronted with paratextual material that indicates the books' connection to the logics of television series. Before reaching the title page, one needs to go through around 40 pages with text and images, which are presented by the headline "New This Season" and may be compared to television's trailers and prequels. All volumes are, for instance, introduced with a section of a story entitled "Astral Omega," which takes place in a distant future, and with stories from an equally distant prehistoric era. These stories function as series within the series and are seemingly unrelated to the main story in *The Familiar*, although hints to possible connections do occur as the series progresses. All volumes conclude with a teaser for the next volume, for instance, in volume 4: "Coming Soon. The Familiar 5. The season one finale. Fall 2017."[8] The volumes furthermore close with several pages of "credits": names of people, translators, designers, layouters, and others who have assisted in the production of the book. This emphasis on collective production also suggests a connection to the logics of television production, which is commonly associated with collaborative creativity, contrasting with the usual conception of a novel as one author's work.[9]

"A different kind of pace."

The emphasis on collectivity is also reflected in the multi-stringed narrative form of the novel, which recalls the structure of many modern television series. *The Familiar* focuses on nine different characters, each related to different plotlines. The central story is about the 12-year-old girl Xanther, who lives in Los Angeles and finds a mysterious small cat in volume 1. This seemingly simple story is complicated, as it is related to other mysterious events taking place around the globe. Besides Xanther, we follow her mother Astair and her stepfather Anwar, the gang leader Luther, the Turkish police officer Özgür, the Armenian taxi driver Shnorhk, the drug addict jingjing in Singapore, the Mexican traveler Isandòrno, and the computer specialist Cas in Texas. Their stories are narrated in different chapters, and each character's chapters are marked with a specific color and typography. For instance, Xanther's chapters are written in the typeface Minion, and are marked with the color pink, while jingjing's chapters are written in rotis semi sans and marked with blue.[10] Toward the ending of each volume, there is a list of which typography belongs to which character. The different characters' stories make up separate plotlines. As noted by Inge van de Ven, this multi-stringed form of narrative recalls so-called "global network films" such as *Traffic* (2000), *Crash* (2004), and *Babel* (2006)—or literary dittos, such as David Mitchell's *Cloud Atlas* (2004).[11] These works all tell the separate stories of characters, who sporadically are brought into contact with each other. In *The Familiar*, the different plotlines are gradually connected, for instance, as some of the characters chew the same kind of gum, participate in the same public events, or use the same social medium, the so-called "Solosphere." Van de Ven concludes that *The Familiar* "dramatizes a social network."[12]

Although the multi-stringed narrative form may also be found in non-serialized works, the serial format stresses the process of gradually weaving together the different plotlines. This process culminates in volume 5 as most of the characters are brought together and a larger plot is partly revealed. The novel at this stage arguably moves beyond the decentered structure of the social network and instead presents a process of building familiarity.[13] Danielewski himself introduces this concept. Commenting on his emphasis on the nuclear family, Xanther and her parents, he notes,

> But the family is larger than that, as you know. It incorporates characters that are beyond the family unit and forces us to look at the entire world in a more familiar way. We have to move away from this kind of estrangement that allows for phenomena like Brexit, or Trump, you know—the ascendancy of people who prey on difference and

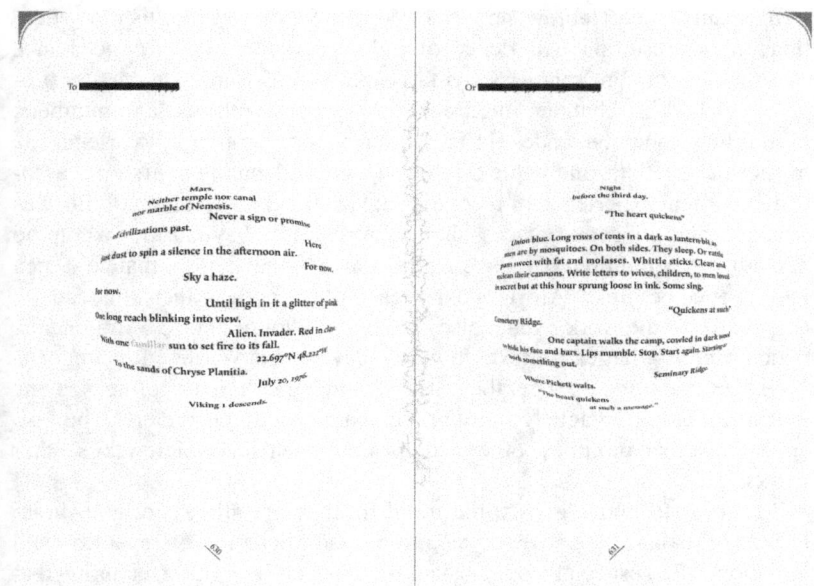

Figure 2.1 Typographical experiments. Illustration from THE FAMILIAR, VOLUME 1: ONE RAINY DAY IN MAY by Mark Z. Danielewski, copyright © 2015 by Mark Z. Danielewski. Used by permission of Pantheon Books, an imprint of the Knopf Doubleday Publishing Group, a division of Penguin Random House LLC. All rights reserved.

strangeness, instead of recognizing that these things are familiar. And if they're not, the book itself is a project of familiarizing people with what Arabic looks like; it's not that scary. With what Armenian looks like; it's not that scary.[14]

Danielewski thus, optimistically, relates the process of connecting characters in his series to a political project of embracing and representing diversity. He furthermore connects this process to the novel's experimental form and presents it as an attempt to "familiarize" readers with foreign languages and forms of expression.

Despite this attempt to build familiarity, *The Familiar*, at first glance, appears radically unfamiliar. The work is marked by experiments with typography and layout, and by what Danielewski calls a "sign iconic" mode of representation: Where textual signs are used to produce visual images.[15]

The work furthermore contains passages in, for example, Chinese, Russian, Spanish, and Hebrew, and in the Singapore dialect Singlish. A reflection on the resulting experience of indecipherability is introduced in a chapter focusing on Xanther's stepfather Anwar. Anwar is a computer programmer and his chapters often contain passages with text and numbers, resembling computer code. He is reading a code written by a friend, the mysterious Mefisto, and while the code appears alienating at first, it is associated with an experience of recognition: "[as much as *so* much of this was strange ⸨pieces beyond pieces ⟨hinting at a whole beyond the (whole no assembly ever required) Anwar couldn't shake the feeling . . . that he'd seen all this once before."[16] Anwar's experience of the code reflects the reader's experience of the work, which also consists of a lot of "pieces," fragments, which hint at a larger context, "a whole beyond the whole." Reading *The Familiar*, one often does get the sense of "having seen it all before," as one is confronted with vaguely familiar elements or with characters, who also appear in other plotlines, other volumes, or even in Danielewski's other works.[17]

As Umberto Eco suggests, the serial form of narration is often characterized by balancing between recognition and alienation or repetition and variation.[18] Eco especially emphasizes the aspect of repetition, claiming that "the series consoles us (the consumers) for our ability to foresee: we are happy because we discover our own ability to expect what will happen."[19] He here refers to classic series in popular culture, such as soaps, which are dominated by a repetitive narrative structure. *The Familiar* is far from repetitive but instead introduces the aspect of recognition as the reader is confronted with familiar elements, such as references to the author's other works or popular television series, and with recognizable patterns such as the typographic keys to the characters or the color-coded chapters.[20] Danielewski links this aspect of the work to its serial format and the theme of building familiarity, claiming that the serial format allows readers gradually see through the experimental form of the novel. "For people who read the first one, it's too opaque, too nonsensical. But then, as you move further and further along, the form itself begins to vanish."[21] Thus, ideally, readers learn to decode the typographical keys and multiple languages as the series progresses.

This hope may, of course, seem rather optimistic. While a few readers in the Facebook group dedicated to the series do describe this experience of becoming familiar with the novel and its experimental esthetics, its overall reception—and the fact that it was eventually paused—reflects that it is generally experienced as difficult, close to illegible. Far from offering the kind of repetitive series described by Eco, it instead reflects a tendency toward narrative complexity described by Jason Mittel. Mittel, as mentioned, traces this tendency in modern television series, pointing to more complex narrative structure in many series and to frequent experimentation with temporality and meta-referentiality.[22] *The Familiar* exemplifies how this tendency also appears in contemporary literature. Danielewski thus uses the serial format to complicate a seemingly simple story about a girl who finds a cat, telling this story with a "different kind of pace" as described in the previous quote. He does so, partly by remediating modern television series, presenting a story with multiple plotlines, and framing it as a television series. However, he also complicates the story and develops the serial dimension by playing with the medium and materiality of the printed book.

Bookishness and Serial Duration

On the backs of all five volumes in the *Familiar* series, two yellow lines can be seen just below the title. On the back of volume 1, the two lines meet and form a bow. When looking at each volume separately, these yellow lines look like a graphic detail, but when the five volumes are placed together on a bookshelf, the lines put together make up what many readers guess is the ending of a cat's tail: A reference to Xanther's small white cat. The rest of the cat was expected to have appeared on the backs of the remaining 22 volumes, had they been published. This graphic detail exemplifies how Danielewski uses the serial format to work with the visuality and materiality of the printed book and, thus, with the series' "shelveability," a concept which Mittell developed in relation to television series in DVD-box-format.[23] The concept refers to the series' quality as a physical collector's object: as more than merely a digital file, or for that matter, a newspaper feuilleton from the 19th century. Mittell describes how 19th-century novels gained the status of lasting and canonized works only once they had been published as finite, "shelveable" works:

> The serial publishing of Dickens and Tolstoy certainly garnered these authors both popularity and acclaim, but had they not been bundled and compiled into published novels, *Bleak House* and *War and Peace* would probably be regarded less as timeless masterpieces and more as ephemerally tied to their historical moment, if remembered at all.[24]

The shelveable book is thus associated with the idea of a durability that reaches beyond the ephemerality commonly associated with serial publishing in other media. *The Familiar* translates this aspect of shelveability back to the world of literature. The books in the series all appear as dense, lasting, and finite objects, which demand not only to be read but also to be handled and looked at. Placed together on a bookshelf, they perform a monumental bookish seriality. This visual aspect was emphasized when Danielewski launched a competition in the *Familiar* Facebook group in 2017, awarding a signed copy of the new volume 5 for the reader, who would take the best picture of the five volumes, all collected.

Thus, while *The Familiar* appears as the product of modern digital culture, inspired by television series, the series also draws attention to the materiality and visuality of printed books, as do Danielewski's other works.[25] Accordingly, it may be considered to exemplify what Jessica Pressman calls the "aesthetics of bookishness"; a tendency in 21st-century literature where printed novels react to digitalization by drawing attention to the visual and material qualities of printed books.[26] In this context, the title of Danielewski's book series may also refer to the book itself as a medium, which becomes important in the digital age as a familiar object and a guarantor of durability and continuity. The book series is thus, first and foremost, presented as a highly shelveable work, associated with a physical and literary density, which is opposed to the sense of immateriality and speed commonly associated with social media and digital technologies. Danielewski emphasizes this contrast in an interview where he describes *The Familiar* as a serial object. He says:

> Really, it's about how we have a conversation with the sensation of time that exceeds a decade. Your lifetime might last somewhere around a century. You're building a family, or starting a company, and it takes decades. And if you're just on Twitter and Instagram experiencing these momentary things, you're going to be deprived of how to understand something that's in a much larger scale.[27]

Danielewski suggests that the series as a narrative format represents a sense of duration, as opposed to the logics of social media that function in and emphasize the moment. It is this "different kind of pace" that he associates with modern television series, as exemplified by *The Wire* in the previous quote. However, I argue that *The Familiar* specifically makes use of the affordances of print to emphasize the idea of serial duration. Already at the level of production, the printed book series contrasts with the model of immediate publishing in social media. Indeed, as a printed book series, the production of *The Familiar* is associated with a process that "exceeds a decade"—from the publication of volume 1 in 2014 to 2027, when volume 27 would have been published had the series not been paused.

The aspect of duration is extended to the level of narration as the serial format is used to literally draw out the telling of the seemingly simple story about a girl who finds a cat.[28] As indicated by the title of volume 1, *One*

"*A different kind of pace.*" 23

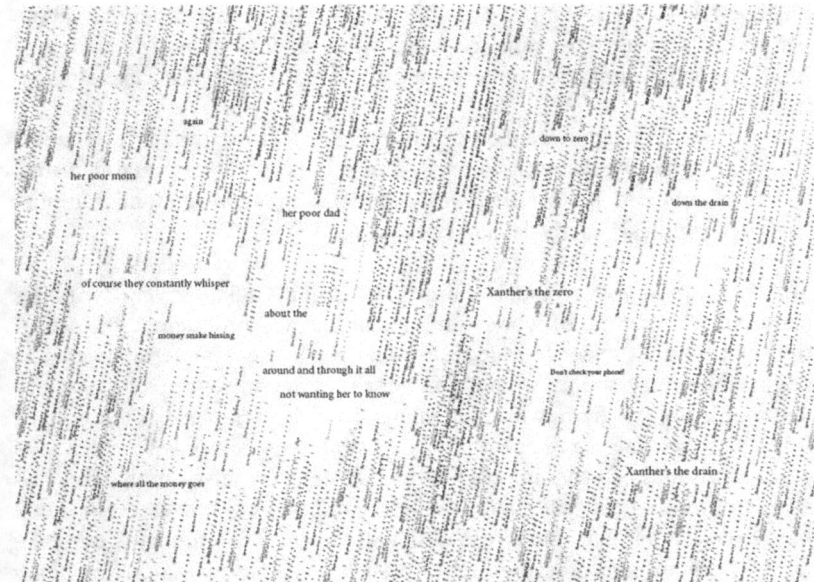

Figure 2.2 Typographical rain. Image from *The Familiar*. Illustration from THE FAMILIAR, VOLUME 1: ONE RAINY DAY IN MAY by Mark Z. Danielewski, copyright © 2015 by Mark Z. Danielewski. Used by permission of Pantheon Books, an imprint of the Knopf Doubleday Publishing Group, a division of Penguin Random House LLC. All rights reserved.

Rainy Day in May, the volume's 880 pages describe events taking place in just one day, reflecting the kind of slow pacing that Danielewski associates with serial storytelling. The typographical and multimodal experiments further contribute to slow down the telling—and reading—of the story. The titular rainstorm, in volume 1, *One Rainy Day in May*, is, for instance, represented with letters and words raining down on the page. The typographical image reflects Xanther's experience of the rain, as she is overwhelmed by the question "how many rain drops?" and results in a pausing of the story, as the reader is equally overwhelmed. *The Familiar* consequently takes a long time to read not only because of the sheer monumentality of the project, many volumes, and pages but also because its experimental form requires a process of careful deciphering and rereadings. Notably, these experiments draw attention to the visual surface of the printed book, and the aspect of duration becomes specifically linked to the work's performance of serial bookishness.

The aspect of duration is furthermore reflected upon in the novel at a diegetic level, when Xanther's mother, Astair, talks to her supervisor about her master's thesis in psychology. Astair wants to write about "the necessity of invention in production of personality,"[29] but the supervisor exclaims,

> You would need more than eighty-one pages, Mrs. Ibrahim. Volumes! And rather than mere volumes—and this is a "rather" qualified man times over—I behold *lifetimes! Lifetimes* of interrogation, examination, synthesis, analysis, and summation.[30]

The Familiar is exactly such a big project which takes several volumes and almost a lifetime of work to tell a story, again, producing "the sensation of time that exceeds a decade." The work uses the serial format to connect the story about Xanther and her cat in the present to a larger story and to a historical framework that spans from the "prequels" taking place in prehistoric times to the posthuman "Astral Omega" stories, which take place thousands of years into the future. Danielewski also emphasizes this aspect of duration in relation to reading and book culture. In a Facebook post from winter 2017, he writes about "the pleasure in thoughts that take time," in relation to other book series, such as Knausgaard's *My Struggle* (he posted an image of the work together with the comment). *My Struggle* and other series such as Elena Ferrante's Neapolitan novels and J.K. Rowling's *Harry Potter* are characterized by the fact that they develop the story over a long time, allowing characters as well as readers to grow with it. Danielewski develops this principle to extremity, as the 27-volume project demands, if not lifetimes of dedication from readers as well as the author, then at least many years of "interrogation, examination, synthesis, analysis, and summation."

Performing bookish seriality, *The Familiar* thus demands the kind of deep attention and dedicated interpretation which is traditionally associated with literary reading and with the culture that surrounds the printed book. "We're book people!" it says in a post in the Facebook reading group, from a reader who wants to know what kind of books the other readers are reading.[31] As the answers to the aforementioned post suggest, they also share a taste for the kind of experimental literature that *The Familiar* exemplifies. Contrary to the series described by Eco, which "consoles" the broad audiences with predictability, this complex narrative builds familiarity in the sense that it speaks to a dedicated niche audience. Danielewski himself contributes to producing this sense of shared literary identity when he posts images of other books and encourages literary discussions, and the work thus gathers people, who familiarize themselves around a collective identity as "book people."

"A different kind of pace." 25

This interaction does, notably, take place on Facebook, on a page where readers also discuss who should play Anwar in a potential television adaptation, which music should be used as a soundtrack, and how images in *The Familiar* remind them of *Stranger Things*. The readers may identify as book people, but the reading culture, which surrounds the series, is framed by the logics of social media and similar to the kind of participatory fan cultures that surround many television series. As I further explore in Chapter 6 of this book, serial narratives are explicitly linked to participatory culture. Serial narratives have a long history of turning reading into a social activity since the waiting time between each installment allows readers to discuss the course of action and even to participate in the continuing construction of the story through communication with the authors. Since serial publication is a continuing process, serial narratives do invite participation in several ways: "Seriality can extend—and normally *does* extend—the sphere of storytelling into the sphere of story consumption," notes Kelleter.[32] Charles Dickens's novels in the 19th century were already surrounded by active and engaged readers who discussed the continued story and tried to affect their development through letters to the author.[33] While social reading has thus always been a part of serial culture, recent years have seen a broader turn toward participatory culture, as discussed by Henry Jenkins. Linking this development to the logic of media convergence, Jenkins notes how "consumption has become a collective process. None of us can know everything; each of us knows something, and we can put the pieces together if we pool our resources and combine our skills."[34] Jenkins focuses on the cultures of participation that surround television series and film, but *The Familiar* illustrates how a similar collective approach may also be found in contemporary literary culture. Later, I thus trace the forms of participatory engagement that surround *The Familiar*.

Building Serial Relations

Online reader communities have also surrounded Danielewski's other works, *House of Leaves* and *Only Revolutions*.[35] However, *The Familiar*'s serial format more explicitly encourages participatory engagement. Danielewski comments on the serial project that "literature is capable of being a subject that people want to catch up on or discuss, whether at a coffee shop or a water cooler,"[36] and his editor, Edward Kastenmeier notes how *The Familiar* is supposed to enter into a "serial relation" with the readers, who may discuss the story continually, between volumes.[37] The Facebook group "The Familiar (volumes 1–5) Reading Club" is an example of how social media shape this serial relation between the work, its readers, and the author, who often participate in, and controls, the discussions on the site.[38]

Notably, the reading culture that surrounds *The Familiar* cannot be limited to the Facebook group, which consists of about 1,500 members. Far from all readers are active, even though works such as *The Familiar* encourage such engagement.[39] Nevertheless, I focus on the Facebook group to examine how the way we read new literary serials is shaped by the logics of social media and by the kind of fan cultures that we know from other media cultures.[40]

Th *Familiar* Facebook page reflects how the series is surrounded by different kinds of reader activities.[41] As it is updated continuously, it may furthermore demonstrate how these activities are defined by the rhythm of the series, as the function of the Facebook page arguably changes, depending on where we are in the process of publication—whether a new volume has just been published, or we are between episodes, or by a season finale. The latter was the case when *The Familiar* volume 5 came out in autumn 2017. During the days preceding the publication, the Facebook page seemed to have a *social function* primarily, as the users, many of whom had not been active since the publication of volume 4, started to share with each other their enthusiasm over the forthcoming volume. As mentioned in my introduction, several images of the newly bought copies were posted in the group, along with images of their cats or other related artifacts. Danielewski was very active on the page and participated in discussions about the work with his readers. Thus, the Facebook group reflects how social media pave the way for a direct—if not familiar—relation between readers and authors.[42]

The social function of the Facebook group dominated until around one week after the publication of volume five when most readers had begun to read the novel. Hereafter, it became the center for an extensive *analytical engagement*. The group is presented as a "reading group" and, to a larger extent than ordinary fan pages, focuses on analytical discussions, which are systemized according to specific page interval, so that the group would read the whole book together throughout November and discuss it as they move through the same passages. The discussions were organized by Danielewski, who posted weekly questions for readers of the week's page interval. Thus, while the credits included in *The Familiar* emphasize a collective process of production, similar to the production of television series, Danielewski still assumed the role of a literary author, who is in control as the one who puts out the questions and encourages interaction on the part of the readers.

The Familiar, in general, encourages collaboration and analytical engagement as its many codes, passages in foreign languages, references, and so forth demand that readers research and collaborate in order to decode the meaning of it all. The publication strategy surrounding the work further encourages this kind of engagement. Before the publication of volume 1, Danielewski organized that selected readers should collaborate on decoding specific pieces of texts, which later became a part of the so-called "Astral

Omega" series within the printed series. In this way, he encouraged the formation of a dedicated reader community and a sense of co-creation in relation to the work, even before it was published. Furthermore, he published the short story "Clip 4" in 2012 in the journal *Black Clock*. The short story functions as a kind of background material for the series and is often mentioned in *The Familiar*. With this kind of "extra material," readers are encouraged to trace connections between the different publications, both within and beyond the printed series. The Facebook page accordingly reflects what Mittell calls *forensic fandom*, a collective, analytical engagement in a given work.[43] In relation to *Familiar* volume 5, this kind of participation was predominant in November 2017, as the reading group read through the novel and helped each other translate passages in foreign languages, trace references, and present theories about the overall plot. Hereafter, the Facebook page became once again marked by social activities, for example, votes about which other books they should read together, and thank-yous to the author for the reading experience.

Apart from the social and analytical engagement, the reading culture surrounding *The Familiar* is also characterized by a *co-creative engagement*. Danielewski involves his readers in the creation of the work, for instance, by asking them to provide feedback via the Facebook group (a few readers are even credited in the books) and by including crowdsourced material in the work. Each volume contains one page with photographs of the readers' cats. The photographs introduce the familiar in the novel; specifically, the photographs look like something we might see on Facebook.

Social media have an important part to play in relation to promoting participatory engagement. Although literary series have always been surrounded by participatory culture, new media have changed the conditions for such engagement. Claire Squires and Padmini Ray Murray describe how readers in digital media culture become "prosumers," that is, co-producers of the narratives in question.[44] This development toward a more active, participating reader or user is often considered a positive democratizing process. Specifically, in relation to serial narratives, Frank Kelleter emphasizes how readers get a larger degree of freedom to influence the narrative: "If a serial narrative can adjust itself to its ongoing reception, serial audiences, in turn, possess more freedom than work audiences to impact the stories they consume."[45] However, it is worth mentioning that the participatory culture surrounding the series is also associated with a commercial aspect, an aspect which is often downplayed by Jenkins and others. Danielewski encourages participation to sell books.[46] His publishing of background material to *The Familiar*, such as the short story "Clip 4," functions as an advertisement for the forthcoming book series. The series is furthermore used as a point of departure to sell things other than books: Danielewski's posts with questions for readers are often concluded with a link to his webpage, where he sells various forms of merchandise, bronze-statues of cats, and t-shirts and bags with printed quotes from his books. In this way, the literary series does not function in other ways than, for instance, film and television series. Kelleter notes that "serial media embody what may well be the structural utopia of the capitalist production of culture at large: the desire to practice reproduction *as* innovation and innovation *as* reproduction."[47] The series functions because it sells "more of the same": a familiar story which is repeatedly presented anew, in new episodes and seasons and products, and when it finally does end, it is usually because it has stopped selling.

This last principle is illustrated by the events following *The Familiar*'s season 1 finale. Despite his original plan of publishing 27 volumes, Danielewski has been frank about the fact that the continuation of the series would depend on its sales. "[A]s with a TV series, every season marks a moment of vulnerability," he wrote on Facebook in 2017. "Pantheon will look at the sales figures in early 2018 and decide the details about Season 2." In February 2018, he announced that the series had been "paused" because "the number of readers is not sufficient for justifying the cost of continuing."[48] Despite the ambitions to represent literary monumentality and produce "the sensation of time that exceeds a decade," the literary series is thus submitted to the same economic conditions as a Netflix series and does not reach further into the future than sales allow.

Conclusion

In this chapter, I have analyzed *The Familiar* as an example of how contemporary literature reacts to a situation where serialization has become a dominant transmedial cultural practice. The work arguably reflects how printed serial literature is inspired by the complex form of narrative seriality that characterizes modern television series, according to Mittell. Furthermore, it reflects how social media logics increasingly influence modern reading culture and how printed serial novels may be surrounded by the same kind of participatory culture that surrounds many television series.

Accordingly, conceived as a project of remediating the serial as well as social and commercial logics of television, *The Familiar* may be considered to reflect a situation discussed by Jim Collins, who argues that serial narratives are no longer medium-specific.[49] He suggests that, since television series become increasingly literary, the traditional hierarchy between the arts has dissolved. "The key point is that literary narratives are no longer necessarily literary, at least not in the sense that they are to be found in books."[50] The consequence, according to Collins, is that a new emphasis is placed on the "story"—specifically, long, serial narratives—no matter the medium: "The print or image-based nature of the medium is no longer the determinant of narrative complexity or its cultural value. Now it's all about 'story' and the delivery system, or more precisely serial stories of indefinite length."[51] Collins explains this development partly as a result of the digital distribution of serial narratives:

> Sophisticated stories of indefinite length are no longer medium specific. . . . The redefinition of the status of extended long format narrative is . . . a direct byproduct of the digital devices on which we consume all of the above. . . . When novels, films, television programs, and songs are all files downloadable from the same sites, all playbackable on the same portable devices, they are all incarnations of the same screen culture.[52]

According to Collins, in the age of Netflix, Twitter, and e-books, the series is no longer medium-specific because we meet it through the same screen, no matter whether it is a television series or a novel. It is, however, possible to question this conclusion. First and foremost, not all serial narratives are distributed via screen, as demonstrated by *The Familiar*. And even those series that are distributed via screen are different from each other, depending on the medium: They are shaped by the affordances of those different media and by the surrounding media cultures. Thus, it does matter whether the story is distributed as an e-book, audiobook, or as a printed novel, both for how the story is produced and narrated and for how it is read or used.

The fact that literary series such as *The Familiar* imitate television series thus does not mean that they are no longer medium-specific. *The Familiar*, on the contrary, exemplifies a literary series specifically shaped by the printed book and for a reading audience. Performing its bookish seriality and translating the kind of "pace" and duration, associated with television series, into a printed series, the novel makes a good case for demonstrating how serial narratives move between the logics of transmediality and medium specificity. In the following chapters of this book, I continue to develop this discussion as I investigate what happens to printed literary series when they are adapted into television series, as in the case of Lemony Snicket's *A Series of Unfortunate Events* and Philip Pullman's *His Dark Materials*, or when the literary series is specifically produced for audiobook or on-screen formats, via platforms such as Storytel or Wattpad.

Certainly, it is possible to criticize this development and consider the current resurgence of the serial format as a reflection of a situation in which literature increasingly needs to compete with Netflix and Facebook. However, it should be stressed that the medial and commercial logics, which surround the series in question, are far from new in the world of literature. Spanning

30 *"A different kind of pace."*

from popular penny dreadfuls to acclaimed novels by Flaubert and Dickens, 19th-century feuilletons also moved across media and platforms such as magazines and newspapers and printed books, and they have always been affected by external factors, such as the readers' loyalty and commercial conditions. Serialization as a transhistorical phenomenon is interesting exactly because of the series' vulnerability to outside intervention, and their possibility to develop beyond the finite frame of the printed book means that they long have been marked by those tendencies which currently, in what Jenkins calls convergence culture, are becoming widespread, also in relation to non-serialized narratives. Book series may thus function as a point of departure for studying how contemporary literature is generally influenced by the logics of media convergence. While the following chapters continue to explore this tendency, the case of *The Familiar* has demonstrated the continuing relevance of the printed book, as it remediates the "pace" and duration of modern television series by performing bookish seriality.

Notes

1. Parts of this chapter are based on the article "'Volumes.' Den litterære serie mellem medier," *Passage* 79 (2018): 117–34. For a discussion of *The Familiar* in comparison to the Storytel Originals series discussed in Chapter 5 of this book, see also Sara Tanderup Linkis, "Literary Remediations of Television Series," in *Television Series as Literature,* eds. Reto Winckler and Victor Huertas-Martín (Shanghai: Palgrave Macmillan, 2021).
2. Danielewski's previous novels, *House of Leaves* and *Only Revolutions,* thus remediate film and music, respectively, while the short *The Fifty Year Sword* reflects on the "campfire story." Alison Gibbons, "Remediation, Storytelling and the Printed Book: The Stylistic Strategies of Mark Z. Danielewski's *the Fifty Year Sword*," in *The Printed Book in Contemporary American Culture*, eds. Heike Schaefer and Alexander Starre (Cham: Palgrave Macmillan, 2019).
3. Mark Z. Danielewski, "The Rumpus Interview with Mark Danielewski," interview by Dylan Foley, *The Rumpus,* May 20, 2015, https://therumpus.net/2015/05/the-rumpus-interview-with-mark-danielewski/.
4. Jason Mittell, *Complex TV. The Poetics of Contemporary Television Storytelling* (New York: New York University Press, 2015); Jim Collins, "The Use Values of Narrativity in Digital Cultures," *New Literary History* 44 (2013): 639–60.
5. Mittel, *Complex TV.*
6. See Jakob Isak Nielsen, "Tv-serien som vor tids roman?" *Passage* 68 (2012): 83–100; Reto Winckler and Victor Huertas-Martín, *Television Series as Literature* (Shanghai: Palgrave Macmillan, 2021).
7. Alison Flood, "Mark Z. Danielewski Wins Seven-Figure Advance for Serial Novel," *The Guardian,* November 22, 2011. The fact that the serialized version of *House of Leaves* in 1999 was compared to the Victorian feuilleton novel, while *The Familiar* in 2014 was primarily compared to the television series, reflects how literature in the 21st century has become increasingly oriented toward the logics of other media and media cultures.

8. Mark Z. Danielewski, *The Familiar 4. Hades* (New York: Pantheon, 2017).
9. On authorship in television series and collaborative production, see Mittell, *Complex TV,* 87–88. In the case of *The Familiar,* it may be discussed how collective this process was. As I describe later, Danielewski stays in control and maintains the authority of a traditional author while claiming that the work is produced collectively and democratically.
10. Chapters narrated from Astair's perspective are marked with orange corners and with the typeface Electra LH, the stepfather Anwar's chapters are marked with green and Adobe Garamond, the gang leader Luther is associated with the color black and Imperial BT, police officer Özgür with gray and Baskerville, Shnorhk with brown and Promemoria, Isandòrno with yellow and Visage, and Cas's chapters are marked with red-brown corners and the typeface Apolline.
11. Inge van de Ven, "The Serial Novel in an Age of Binging. How to Read Mark Z. Danielewski's *the Familiar,*" *Image & Narrative* 17, no. 4 (2016): 91–103.
12. Van de Ven, "Binging," 94. She only comments on the first three volumes, writing before the other volumes had been published. Later, I argue that the serial development of the work means that it moves away from the network structure, especially in volume 5.
13. For a detailed description of the process of building familiarity, see Sara Tanderup Linkis, "The Form Itself Begins to Vanish: Seriality and Multimodality in Mark Z. Danielewski's *the Familiar,*" in *Fictionality and Multimodal Narratives,* eds. Alison Gibbons and Torsa Ghosal (Lincoln and London: University of Nebraska Press, forthcoming).
14. Mark Z. Danielewski, "Building Familiarity," interview by Javier Calvo, *O Magazine,* 2017, https://abcdefghijklmn-pqrstuvwxyz.com/building-familiarity-interview-with-mark-z-danielewski/.
15. Danielewski defines the sign iconic as follows: "Signiconic = sign + icon. Rather than engage those textual faculties of the mind remediating the pictorial or those visual faculties remediating language, the signiconic simultaneously engages both in order to lessen the significance of both, and therefore achieve a third perception no longer dependent on sign and image for remediating a world in which the mind plays no part." Mark Z. Danielewski, "Reading Guide," www.penguinrandomhouse.ca/books/213606/the-familiar-volume-2-by-mark-z-danielewski/9780375714962/reading-guide.
16. Mark Z. Danielewski, *The Familiar 2. Into the Forrest* (New York: Pantheon, 2015), 511.
17. For instance, Cas and her husband are suddenly, in one scene in *The Familiar* volume 4, called by the names of Hailey and Sam, a reference to the protagonists in Danielewski's previous novel *Only Revolutions* (2006).
18. Umberto Eco, *The Limits of Interpretation* (Bloomington and Indianapolis: Indiana University Press, 1994), 83–100.
19. Ibid., 86.
20. For further reflection on this element of recognizability in *The Familiar,* see van de Ven, "Binging."
21. Danielewski, "Building Familiarity."
22. Mittell, *Complex TV.*
23. Ibid., 37.
24. Ibid.
25. This emphasis on the visuality of the book object is supplemented with experiments with smell, in volume 5: Many readers describe how their copies smell of

the titular redwood. The smell does disappear with time and is thus characterized by an ephemerality which contrasts with the impression of a monumental and lasting, finite work.

26. On bookishness, see Jessica Pressman, "The Aesthetics of Bookishness in Twenty-First-Century Literature," *Michigan Quarterly Review* 48 (2009), http://hdl.handle.net/2027/spo.act2080.0048.402; See also Jessica Pressman, *Bookishness. Loving Books in the Digital Age* (New York: Columbia University Press, 2020).
27. Mark Z. Danielewski, "A Conversation with Mark Z. Danielewski," interview by Philbert Dy, *Rogue Books*, 2017, http://rogue.ph/conversation-mark-z-danielewski/.
28. For a more thorough analysis of this, see Tanderup Linkis, "Literary Remediations."
29. Danielewski, *Forrest*, 423.
30. Ibid., 424–25.
31. Anonymized Post, "The Familiar (Volumes 1–5) Reading Club," *Facebook*, November 6, 2017.
32. Frank Kelleter, "From Recursive Progression to Systemic Self-Observation. Elements of a Theory of Seriality," *Velvet Light Trap* 79 (2017): 100.
33. For further discussion of historical serial reading culture, see Jennifer Poole Hayward, *Consuming Pleasures: Active Audiences and Serial Fictions from Dickens to Soap Opera* (Lexington: University Press of Kentucky, 1997).
34. Henry Jenkins, *Convergence Culture. Where Old and New Media Collide* (New York and London: New York University Press, 2006), 26.
35. See Bronwen Thomas, "Trickster Authors and Tricky Readers on the MZD Forums," in *Mark Z. Danielewski*, eds. Joe Bray and Alison Gibbons (Manchester: Manchester University Press, 2011), 86–102.
36. Quoted in Julie Bosman, "Periodical Novel, Coming Soon," *The New York Times*, February 22, 2011, https://mediadecoder.blogs.nytimes.com/2011/11/20/periodic-novel-coming-soon/.
37. Ibid.
38. The social media framing of the reading group and Danielewski's personal involvement in this group may be compared to the communities that surround Danielewski's previous works, which take place on specialized online forums. Reflecting the fact that these forums are based on anonymity, as described by Thomas, "Trickster Authors," Danielewski is not present in these forums and rather appears as a mysterious and absent author figure.
39. For a discussion of the limitations of participatory culture, see Tore Rye Andersen and Sara Tanderup Linkis, "As We Speak. Concurrent Narration and Participation in the Serial Narratives *Skam* and '@I_Bombaldil'," *Narrative* 27, no. 1 (2019): 83–106.
40. The reader culture surrounding *The Familiar* does, in fact, seem to be even more dependent on social media than the reader culture that surrounds television series because Danielewski's experimental novel is more of a niche product. Several members of the *Familiar* Facebook group thus comment on the fact that they do not know anyone in "real life" who reads "that kind of books." Rather than discussing the work by the water cooler at the workplace, such as Danielewski suggests, it is obvious to use Facebook and other online platforms to connect with other readers.

41. See Andersen and Linkis, "As We Speak," for a typology over forms of participation that surround digitally distributed serials. See van de Ven, "Binging," for a discussion of the participatory culture that surrounds the first volumes of *The Familiar*.
42. For more on the relation between authors and readers in digital culture, see, e.g., Claire Squires and Padmini Ray Murray, "The Digital Publishing Communications Circuit," *Book 2.0* 3, no. 1 (2013): 3–24.
43. Jason Mittell, "Sites of Participation. Wiki Fandom and the Case of Lostpedia," *Transformative Works and Cultures* 3 (2009).
44. Murray and Squires, "Digital Publishing."
45. Kelleter, "Theory of Seriality," 101. Kelleter notes how this freedom for the reader implies potential "authorization conflicts," since active and participating readers challenge the author or the publisher's control of the story. In relation to *The Familiar*, it should, however, be stressed that Danielewski remains in control, since he himself frames the kinds of reader activities that surround the work.
46. Notably, the books are not cheap! In this way, Danielewski's series does differ from the 19th- century feuilletons, which were indeed published as feuilletons in order to make them accessible for people who could not afford to buy the bound volumes. In the case of *The Familiar*, every episode in the series is a carefully designed book object.
47. Kelleter, "Theory of Seriality," 104.
48. Readers reacted to Danielewski's comments by coordinating approaches to Pantheon in order to secure the continuation of the series, further reflecting the participatory aspect of serial culture.
49. Jim Collins, "Fifty Shades of Seriality and E-Readers Games," *Akademisk Kvarter* 7 (2013): 366–79.
50. Collins, "Use Values," 651.
51. Ibid., 652.
52. Collins, "Fifty Shades," 374–75.

3 "The End is really the middle of the story." Transmedial Seriality in Lemony Snicket's *A Series of Unfortunate Events*

"Now a Netflix original series!" proclaims a note from publisher Harper-Collins on the first four-volume "Netflix Tie-In Box Set" of *A Series of Unfortunate Events*.[1] The note demonstrates how the recent adaptation (2017–19) of the popular novels by Lemony Snicket (alias Daniel Handler) into a television series literally marks the printed books. The Netflix reference is even more noticeable as it clashes with the otherwise bookish design of the Snicket series. The books imitate a traditional Victorian book design, with marbled endpapers and numerous illustrations by Brett Helquist. The fabric binding the pages to the spine of each volume is presented in bright colors that match Helquist's front cover illustrations, presenting a series of beautiful, matching, and highly "shelveable" books.[2]

In this way, like Danielewski's *The Familiar*, *A Series of Unfortunate Events* already emphasizes its serial format at a material level. While *The Familiar* represented an attempt to reinvent the serial format through a bookish experiment, the design of the Snicket books suggests a connection to the tradition of Victorian serial literature. The Netflix sticker, furthermore, reflects how the work relates to seriality as a transmedial form of storytelling in contemporary culture. As its successful publication followed that of J. K. Rowling's Harry Potter series in the late 1990s to the early 2000s, *A Series of Unfortunate Events* is an obvious example of how serialization has become a widespread mode of telling and selling children's literature. This chapter accordingly investigates the use of seriality in *A Series of Unfortunate Events*, both as a principle of narrative organization within the book series and as a strategy of transmedial storytelling.

The first part of the chapter focuses on the narrative development in the book series. *A Series of Unfortunate Events* has been criticized for its repetitive serial structure—for expanding the story merely for the sake of commercial exploitation. I argue, however, that the series advances beyond repetition, gradually complicating the serial narrative both within the books and when it moves across media. As indicated by its title, *A Series* of *Unfortunate Events* is characterized by serial self-reflexivity, continuously commenting on its own status as a series and a commodity. I argue that through this self-reflexivity and its increasing narrative complexity, the series promotes an active, critical reception rather than passive consumption of "more of the same" story.

The work's development across media further complicates the story. Drawing, once again, on Jason Mittell's concept of "complex television" and emphasizing the idea of transmedia storytelling as theorized by Henry Jenkins, I analyze how the television adaptation extends the narrative complexity of the novels. In this way, I develop the argument presented in Chapter 2: While *The Familiar* appears as a remediation of television series within a printed book series, this chapter focuses on what I call *transmedial complexity*: how the story is complicated as the series is developed across media. Thus, by analyzing the narrative development of *A Series of Unfortunate Events*, it is possible to shed new light on the series as a transforming and transmedial form of storytelling in contemporary culture.

Seriality and Repetition

A Series of Unfortunate Events at first glance appears to exemplify Umberto Eco's association of the series with repetition, also invoked in Chapter 2. "To serialize means, in some way, to repeat,"[3] writes Eco. He defines seriality as a broad category that includes such phenomena as remakes, reboots, and even intertextuality. This description seems to fit well with Snicket's *A Series of Unfortunate Events*, which is dominated by a narrative repetitive scheme. The title itself invokes the notion of the series in order to emphasize the repeated misfortune of its three child protagonists, Violet, Klaus, and Sunny Baudelaire, who lose their parents in a house fire in the first chapter of book 1, *The Bad Beginning*. The children inherit a fortune and are placed under the care of a distant relative, the actor Count Olaf, who turns out to be a greedy villain. In the first book, he attempts to steal the children's fortune by imprisoning baby Sunny in a birdcage and threatening to kill her unless Violet marries him. As his evil scheme is revealed toward the end of the book, everything is set for a happy ending, but Olaf escapes and continues to pursue the children and their fortune throughout the rest of the series. The next five books are characterized by a formulaic structure: At the beginning of each novel, the children are placed under the care of a new guardian. Olaf turns up in disguise, causing great misery, and Violet, Klaus, and Sunny manage to escape and expose his evil scheme only by using their personal skills—and a lot of books.

Clarisse Loughrey describes what she calls the "almost fairytale-like sense of cyclical repetition" in the books as a "structural approach that offered two sensations: first, a feeling of warm familiarity, akin to sinking oneself into a favorite armchair. Second, the incurable sensation of despair felt by the Baudelaires, unable to free themselves from the pattern of devastation."[4] According to Loughrey, Snicket's work at once uses the serial formula to lure the readers to return time and again to the series while also imposing upon them the protagonists' frustration and despair as unhappy history repeats itself. The latter aspect is stressed by Snicket, in his role as a narrator, through repeated ironic warnings to the readers: "If you are interested in stories with happy endings, you would be better off reading some other book," he states on page 1 of *The Bad Beginning*. "In this book, not only is there no happy ending, there is no happy beginning and very few happy things in the middle." In this way, the work uses the concept of seriality to shape the readers' expectations, foreshadowing the orphans' continuous misfortune. Seriality, in this context, becomes associated with the frustrating recognition that there is no escape from bad luck. This aspect of the work has resulted in its categorization as gothic fiction, or rather, as a parody of the gothic novel, since Snicket's darkly humorous narration constantly punctuates the horror and despair with irony.[5]

A Series of Unfortunate Events accordingly relates to Eco's idea of seriality as a form of repetition not only because of its formulaic plot repetitions but also because of its use of parody and intertextuality. Eco defines the latter as a form of repetitive seriality, focusing on those occasions "when the quotation is explicit and recognizable, as happens in postmodern literature and art, which blatantly and ironically play on the intertextuality."[6] *A Series of Unfortunate Events* is filled with such explicit references to literary classics and authors. Just consider the names of such characters as the banker Mr. Poe and the doctor Georgina Orwell, not to mention the Baudelaire orphans themselves. Following Eco, we may describe the Snicket series as an example of postmodern serial fiction characterized by the logic of repetition at a structural and referential level but with a marked irony and meta-reflexivity. Later in this chapter, I discuss how these aspects of the work add to its development of narrative complexity and promote critical engagement. However, the reception of the series has focused less on this dimension of critical reflexivity and more on the repetitive structure as a reflection of a commercial agenda. Bruce Butt claims that repetition "has been at the centre of the series' success."[7] Butt describes repetition as a general characteristic of children's literature and criticizes the Snicket series because its repetitions, according to him, add nothing to the story:

> Whereas J. K. Rowling might argue that she needed seven books to see Harry Potter through Hogwarts, there are no conceptual reasons for the Snicket series to extend over 13 books; only financial ones. Once the

first two have been read and the pattern established, additions to the series could easily be skipped with no barriers to a reader's understanding of plot, character, or context. They have continued merely because they can.[8]

Butt notably presented this criticism before the whole series had been published—he primarily comments on books 1–4. However, the formulaic structure was broken from book 6. As I further explain later, the work transformed from a cyclical series into a more complex narrative, with several plot lines, characters, and relationships developing across the remaining books.

While Butt's criticism of the repetitive structure of the Snicket series may be disputed, he is correct in pointing out the commercial incentives of serial publishing in general and of *A Series of Unfortunate Events* in particular. Evoking Eco's concept of the series as a form of narrative that translates repetition into innovation, Frank Kelleter argues that seriality is essentially a capitalist mode of storytelling. As noted in Chapter 2, he argues that serial media embody "the desire to practice reproduction *as* innovation, and innovation *as* reproduction,"[9] and thus become "prime sites of *capitalist self-reflexivity*."[10] That is because capitalism "functions only under the condition that it creates belief in its continued existence in the future"[11]—and seriality promises continuity. Kelleter concludes, "Serial media reproduce a sense of infinite futurity, without which capitalist market cultures would threaten to collapse at every crisis point."[12] *A Series of Unfortunate Events* illustrates this logic. It reproduces a sense of "infinite futurity" by emphasizing its serial continuation. Each book concludes with an authentic-looking typed letter from Lemony Snicket to his editor, hinting at the unfortunate events to come and thus providing a teaser, making sure that the readers buy the next volume. Furthermore, the series has been expanded beyond the original series. Handler has published several spin-offs, including *Lemony Snicket: The Unauthorized Autobiography* (2002); a collection of fictional letters, *The Beatrice Letters* (2006); and the prequel series *All the Wrong Questions* (2012–15), not to mention the adaptations. The Netflix series is only the most recent manifestation of the books, the first three of which were also adapted into a film by Brad Silberling in 2004. Last but not least, *A Series of Unfortunate Events* has generated merchandise such as "unfortunate" T-shirts, board games, card games, video games, and an album, *The Tragic Treasury*, by Handler's band The Gothic Archies.

A Series of Unfortunate Events thus appears as a commercial serial brand that is developed and sold in its various manifestations across media. The brand is consistently marketed through Snicket's ironic style, resulting in a highly ambiguous promotion. Consider, for instance, the promotional text

38 *"The End is really the middle of the story."*

on HarperCollins's Web site for the 2006 boxed set, *A Series of Unfortunate Events: The Complete Wreck*:

> Some boxes should never be opened. For the first time, the complete A Series of Unfortunate Events is available in one awful package! We can't keep you from succumbing to this international bestselling phenomenon, but we can hide all thirteen books in a huge, elaborately illustrated, shrink-wrapped box, perfect for filling an empty shelf or deep hole.[13]

The text warns the reader about opening the box yet promotes the work as an "international bestselling phenomenon." *A Series of Unfortunate Events* thus exemplifies a commercial use of the serial format; it expands the story in order to sell more; yet exposes a critical self-reflexivity to the extent that the narrator's warnings against reading the work turn into a recognizable brand used to promote the series.

Serial Complexity and Critical Readers

Commenting upon the success of *A Series of Unfortunate Events*, Handler says: "It would really be horrible to be associated with fast food but then not too long ago I had a fantasy that, you know, there would be Unhappy Meals that would come out of *A Series of Unfortunate Events*."[14] The comment displays the author's ambivalence about the series as a commodity. Although tempted by the fantasy of Unhappy Meals, Handler does not want to serve literary fast food to his young readers. Accordingly, his work seeks to distance itself from the commercial logic of seriality by moving beyond the "fast food" stage of mere repetition and toward a level of narrative complexity that encourages critical reflection.[15] I argue that this development may be connected to its presentation of a reversed power balance between the adults and children in the story as well as between the adult narrator and the child readers, as the complex narrative arguably promotes critical awareness and independent readers.

As mentioned earlier, the series' repetitive structure is broken off after book 6. Several plot elements are developed across the remaining books, such as a hint that one of the Baudelaire parents might be alive, the introduction (and kidnapping) of the Baudelaires' friends, the Quagmire triplets, and the continuing emergence of the mysterious letter combination "V. F. D." Furthermore, each book no longer concludes with the restoration of law and order as Olaf's evil schemes are revealed to the world; instead, the story is just broken off, to be continued in the next book. Book 9, *The Carnivorous Carnival*, concludes with a literal cliff-hanger as it leaves Violet and

Klaus trapped inside a wagon that is rolling down a mountain and (almost) off a cliff.[16] The ending of the series contains a meta-reflection on seriality, emphasizing the story's lack of closure. In *The End*, the narrator comments,

> One could say, in fact, that no story really has a beginning, and that no story really has an end. . . . We might even say that the world is in medias res—a Latin phrase which means "in the midst of things" or "in the middle of a narrative"—and that it is impossible to solve any mystery, or find the root of any trouble, and so *The End* is really the middle of the story.[17]

The work, and the world, are considered to be "in medias res," referring to the fact that the series undermines the narrative conventions of a story that require a beginning, a middle part, and a happy ending. This point is underlined by the fact that *The End* does not provide closure; a lot of the mysteries presented throughout the series are left unanswered. We never get a happy ending (or any ending) for the Baudelaire orphans. Instead, the book ends with an epilogue, Chapter 14, which allows us a glimpse of the orphans one year after the events in *The End*—and leaves them as they sail away toward new adventures and beyond the narrative control of the adult narrator. In this way, the development toward a more complex serial structure parallels the development of the child protagonists, who become more independent and gain agency during the series, moving beyond the control of the adults. As the plot formula is broken, they are no longer placed with new guardians at the beginning of each book. They move forward on their own. In this way, they move from being passive victims and heirs to the family fortune, lacking legal capacity, to becoming independent and capable of taking care of themselves.

This development is notably associated with the children's preoccupation with literature. Throughout the series, Violet, Klaus, and Sunny use books to fight Count Olaf and his accomplices, from *The Bad Beginning*—when they escape into the library of Olaf's kind neighbor, Justice Strauss, and Klaus reads up on nuptial law, which helps him reveal Olaf's evil scheme to marry Violet—to *The End*, which features a rescue boat literally made up of books. Furthermore, in *The End*, the children find one special book entitled *A Series of Unfortunate Events*, which was written by their parents and contains the truth about the antidote that will rescue them from a deadly poison. By reading, the children are able to save themselves and expose the schemes of the villainous adults. Through its serial development, moving beyond repetition, the series likewise encourages its young readers to become critical readers, as they mature with the protagonists and, like them, become able to see through Olaf's disguises as well as Snicket's unreliable narration. Therefore, the development of the protagonists and their relation to the villainous adults in the story can be compared to the developing relationship between the narrator and fictional author, Snicket, and the primary target group of child readers.

At first glance, Snicket represents an authoritative adult narrative voice, typical of didactive Victorian children's literature.[18] He acts as the supercilious adult who explains the moral of the story to the readers and defines the meaning of specific words. For instance, he writes, "the word 'phantasmagorical' here means 'all the creepy, scary words you can think of put together'";[19] "transpired, which here means 'happened and made everybody sad'";[20] and "the word 'hackneyed' here means 'used by so, so many writers that by the time Lemony Snicket uses it, it is a tiresome cliché.'"[21] However, as these examples reflect, Snicket's authority as a narrator is undermined as his explanations prove unreliable. Eventually, he loses control of the story. Elizabeth Bullen argues that Lemony Snicket enacts a strategy of "disempowered authority"[22] since he is unable to intervene in the story, just as he is unable to control the readers with his repeated warnings. In this way, the traditional power dynamics between the adult author/narrator and the child reader are subverted. Snicket's status as the fictional author of the series further serves to deconstruct his authority, as Handler uses him to "illustrate how untrustworthy the construction of 'author' really is."[23] The series thus promotes a child reader who is able to see through the adults' disguises—Handler's as well as Olaf's.

Notably, this critical dimension of the work also promotes awareness of the commercial function of the series. As Magnussen argues,

> Handler's invention of Snicket mocks and derides his series' obvious intention to solicit consumption. By implicating the reader directly, Handler/Snicket encourages the self-conscious consumption of literature, as well as of other commodities. Moreover, by creating a "child-friendly" author (Snicket) who is manifest in the text yet impossibly elusive, Handler encourages his young readers to critique authorial manipulation as well as to question the competing constructions of childhood.[24]

A Series of Unfortunate Events thus presents literary engagement and reading as a way to promote critical reflexivity and resist commercial exploitation. This is also true at the diegetic level. Throughout the series, the Baudelaire children's "literary" values are opposed to the greed of the adults—most of them actors—who repeatedly seek to exploit them and steal their fortune. By reading, the children in the books come to see through the unreliable stories and commercial exploitation of the adults.

The series explicitly associates this form of critical awareness with literature and, not least, with physical books, as reflected by the fact that the book *A Series of Unfortunate Events* in *The End* is presented as an effective antidote to deadly poison and commercial exploitation. What happens, then, when the story moves out of the book and into television? I argue that just as the work complicates the traditional power relations between children and adults, and between readers and author, it also complicates the established hierarchy regarding literature and television—and original and adaptation—as the development toward narrative complexity continues in the Netflix adaptation.

"Look away!": Serial Complexity across Media

"Look away, look away," sings Count Olaf in the introductory song for the Netflix production of *A Series of Unfortunate Events*. "This show will wreck your evening, your whole life and your day/ Every single episode is nothing but dismay/So look away."[25] The warning from the books is adjusted to a television audience, as the song emphasizes the activity of (not) looking rather than (not) reading. The song reflects how the adaptation adjusts the story according to the affordances of streaming television while also playing with its connection to the books. Although the Netflix series at first glance appears to be simply a repetition of the book series, I argue that it adds to the work's development toward serial complexity, allowing the story to move beyond mere adaptation as repetition.[26] Not least, this development also serves to expand the target group for Snicket's work, making the series appeal in different ways to different groups of (young and older) viewers and encouraging new modes of consumption across media.

From the beginning, the adaptation continues the development toward narrative complexity that I traced in the book series. Each book is covered by two episodes. Season 1's eight episodes thus cover the first four books, season 2 covers the next five books in ten episodes, and season 3 covers the last four books in seven episodes—*The End* being adapted into just one. The development toward narrative complexity is reflected in the fact that the early episodes already include hints about the Baudelaire parents' pasts and the secret V. F. D. organization, presenting the episodic plots of the first books in the light of the bigger serial plot that is revealed only later in the book series. Furthermore, new plot lines and characters are introduced in the adaptation, building up the back story about the parents. This development toward a more complex serial structure may in part be motivated by the series' adjustment to the medial affordances of streaming television. Loughrey suggests that the differences between the book and the television versions may be linked to the different temporalities of the serially published books and the Netflix series. While the books were separated by their publication dates, justifying the repetitions as readers would return to enjoy the familiar story after a long time, the adaptation has to prevent "boredom from kicking in" in a Netflix culture where whole seasons are often released at once and consumed ("binged") in a few weeks, days, or hours.[27]

However, the transmedial development of *A Series of Unfortunate Events* may also be said to reflect the development toward narrative complexity in 21st-century television, as described by Mittell and also discussed in Chapter 2 of this book. Mittell notes,

> [A] new paradigm of television storytelling has emerged over the past two decades, redefining the boundary between episodic and serial forms, with a heightened degree of self-consciousness in storytelling mechanics, and demanding intensified viewer engagement focused on both diegetic pleasures and formal awareness.[28]

A Series of Unfortunate Events, with its meta-reflexivity and increasingly complex narrative structure, certainly reflects this tendency. Mittell argues that "At its most basic level, narrative complexity *redefines episodic forms under the influence of serial narration*"[29] and explains,

> Rejecting the need for plot closure within every episode that typifies conventional episodic form, narrative complexity foregrounds ongoing stories across a range of genres. Complex television employs a range of serial techniques with the underlying assumption that a series is a cumulative narrative that builds over time, rather than resetting back to steady-state equilibrium at the end of every episode.[30]

While Mittell insists that this development is specific for television, it may also be seen in printed book series, as argued in Chapter 2 in relation to the case of *The Familiar*. The Snicket series, in turn, demonstrates how serial complexity may appear as a product of transmedial interaction. When considered together, the different versions of *A Series of Unfortunate Events* reflect the idea of the series as accumulative narrative that builds over time *across media*: the adaptation develops its narrative complexity by playing with its relationship to the books while also expanding the story by drawing on other related material. Focusing on this aspect paves the way for considering the Snicket series in relation to the concept of transmedial storytelling, defined by Jenkins as "a process where integral elements of a fiction get dispersed systematically across multiple delivery channels for the purpose of creating a unified and coordinated entertainment experience."[31] *A Series of Unfortunate Events* may not be a classic case of transmedia storytelling since it originates in one source text. However, focusing on the serial development of the story makes it relevant to consider the transmedial aspect of that development. I thus examine how the adaptation interacts with—rather than just repeats—the book series, moving toward increasing serial complexity.

The opening credits in the Netflix series already point to its complex relationship to the books. The work is presented as "based on the book series by Lemony Snicket" but also credits the empirical author, Handler, who has written several episodes. The Netflix production is thus presented as a product of the empirical author, who lends authority to the adaptation. The fictional author, Snicket, has also been used to promote the Netflix adaptation; for instance, the renewal of the series for a second season in April 2017 was announced via a letter supposedly written by Snicket:

> It has come to my attention that, despite my repeated warnings, you have viewed the Netflix adaptation of my distressing work, known collectively as *A Series of Unfortunate Events*. Some of you have even binged, a word which here means "watched several episodes in a row, despite having much better things to do with your time." To my horror, Netflix has been encouraged by this and funneled their ill-gotten gains toward a second season of this unhappy and unnerving series.[32]

With his recognizable ironic style, Snicket is used to emphasize the connection between the Netflix series and the books, "known collectively as *A Series of Unfortunate Events*." He has the authority to officially announce the renewal of the series while also staging his powerlessness before Netflix's decision to continue the story, acting as the disempowered author who has lost control of his work, which has become subject to commercial exploitation, with Netflix "funneling their ill-gotten gains" toward its continuation. Snicket's warning is used to promote the adaptation while also ironically commenting on its status as a commodity and reflecting on the fact that Handler has, in fact, lost his authority as the original author in relation to the series and become a writer in the production team behind the Netflix series.

While using Snicket in this paratextual way to emphasize its connection to the books, the Netflix series also repeatedly reflects on its status as a commercial television production. This aspect further connects it to Mittell's notion of complex television. According to Mittell, complex television series are often characterized by self-referentiality and narrative special effects: that is, "when a program flexes its storytelling muscles to confound and amaze a viewer."[33] He further notes,

> These moments of spectacle push the operational aesthetic to the foreground, calling attention to the narration's construction and asking us to

marvel at how the writers pulled it off; often these instances forgo strict realism in exchange for a formally aware baroque quality in which we watch the process of narration as a machine rather than engaging in its diegesis.[34]

The Snicket books, of course, already feature such self-referential elements as they draw attention to the process of narration when the narrator comments on the narrative structure of the work or addresses the readers directly. The adaptation adjusts this self-referential aspect to the medium of television as the narrator, Snicket (played by Patrick Warburton), is often present on screen, stepping in front of the camera while the characters freeze around him. He breaks the fourth wall as he addresses the viewers, thus interrupting the showing of events by drawing attention to his telling of them.

However, the television series also takes this self-referential aspect to a new level as not only the narrator but also the characters comment on the narrative and medial construction of the series, subtly referring to the fact that the story is presented in a television series on a streaming platform. Count Olaf especially becomes associated with this uncanny effect. For instance, in "The Bad Beginning—Part Two," Olaf, on his way to perform in a play in which he intends to marry Violet, pronounces to the press, "I think live theater is a much more powerful medium than, say, streaming television."[35] Furthermore, in episode 3, "The Reptile Room—Part One," when the children plan to go to the movies with their new guardian, Olaf, in disguise, comments, "I prefer long-form television to the movies. It's so much more convenient to consume entertainment from the comfort of your own home."[36] He then turns to stare directly into the camera, facing the viewers with a sinister grin. In this way, Olaf gives the impression of being well aware of his performance in a television series, adding to the latter's uncanny effect.

The serial organization of the show, in seasons and episodes, is also emphasized by the characters. For instance, at the end of the season 1 finale, Count Olaf asks the children if they have not learned anything "This year? This week? This season?"[37]—confusing different levels of time in the series by referring not only to the year, which may have passed within the story world during season 1 (the "story time"), but also to the season having passed at the level of narration (the "discourse time"), as well as to the week it may take to watch the eight episodes in season 1 (the "screen time").[38] According to Mittell, such foregrounding of serial temporality is quite common in contemporary television: "Complex television programs invite temporary disorientation and confusion, allowing viewers to build up their comprehension skills through long-term viewing and active engagement."[39] Following Mittell, we may conclude that by "flexing its storytelling muscles," reflecting on the medium of television and referring to its serial structure, the Netflix series encourages viewers to reflect on its ongoing narrative construction.

In this case, however, the "active engagement" mentioned by Mittell may involve not only watching the television series but also reading the books and reflecting on the different versions of the work. The adaptation invites this kind of engagement by subtly commenting on its relation to the book series. For instance, at the beginning of episode 7, "The Miserable Mill—Part One," the banker Mr. Poe, upon discovering that the Baudelaire children have sneaked away while he was confronting Count Olaf, cries out, "It's a catastrophe! It's unprecedented! It's off-book! It's unfortunate!"[40] The book series is at this stage in the story still marked by the repetitive structure, and Poe himself takes the Baudelaires to the Lucky Smells Lumber Mill to meet their new guardian; in the adaptation, however, the children go to the mill on their own. Poe's cry of "It's off-book!" thus refers to the fact that the series has literally gone away from the books.

In this way, the Netflix series rewards those viewers who engage in the different versions of the story. This becomes evident when considering how the adaptation plays with its relation to the books by presenting a new plotline that unfolds during the first season, adding to the story's transmedial complexity. That is, from episode 1, the familiar story from the books about the three children enduring Count Olaf's cruelties is juxtaposed with scenes presenting two adults breaking out of prison. It is understood that they seek to get back to their children, leading viewers to assume that they are the Baudelaire parents, alive after all. Those viewers who have read the books are led to speculate about how this new plot line relates to the story in the books, in which the Baudelaire parents remain dead (despite speculation to the contrary midway through the series). This game of expectations reaches a climax in the season 1 finale, where we are led to expect that the children and the adults will finally meet. The Baudelaire children, who stay at the Lucky Smells Lumber Mill, are told that someone wants to meet them at the mill's big, yellow door. The series makes a cut to the parents, who are also approaching a yellow door, leading us to expect that the children will meet their parents upon opening it. However, these expectations are undermined when the parents open the door, shouting the names of three other children, while the Baudelaires, behind their door, find no one but Count Olaf in a new disguise.[41] Thus, the adaptation, in the end, remains true to the books. Rather than changing the central premises of the story, the adaptation diverges from the books only to play with viewers' expectations. Instead of repeating the story in the books, the adaptation complicates it by adding new plot lines, causing viewers to become uncertain about its continuing development, allowing them to hope for a happy ending—and finally confronting them with the fact that they were tricked when this hope is disappointed after all. Even when it departs from the books, the adaptation thus remains true to the elements of suspense and disillusion that characterize the books. Paradoxically, through its very divergence from the books, it succeeds in provoking the same gothic effect.

This play with the variations between books and television series can be fully appreciated only by those viewers who have read the books, leading to the division of the audience into two categories—those who have read the books and those who are new to the story. Because of the time gap between the publication of the books in the early 2000s and the release of the Netflix series in 2017, most of the readers-turned-viewers will be young adults, returning to the series that they may have read in their childhood, while many newcomers may be children (considering Netflix's promotion of the series as children's entertainment).[42] Notably, this division in the audience may be compared to the division produced by the book series between those readers who recognize the literary references in the work and those who do not notice them. Like most children's literature, the book series is already characterized by a double address, speaking to both children and adults. The process of serialization emphasizes this aspect because the readers may grow up as the story unfolds both serially and across media. Linda Hutcheon suggests that "Readers literally go from innocence to experience over the course of a narrative, and certainly in moving from an adapted text to an adaptation, they become 'knowing' readers, no longer presumed innocent."[43] As demonstrated previously, the narrative development of *A Series of Unfortunate Events* emphasizes this process, representing the protagonists as they grow up through reading and as we read. Arguably, the series encourages a similar development in its readers, who become "knowing" readers and viewers as the story develops across media.

However, while the Netflix series addresses readers-turned-viewers, it also attracts newcomers who may move in the opposite direction, from watching the adaptation to reading the books. This perspective allows us to return to the Netflix sticker on the book cover, promoting the books through the adaptation. Other new editions have replaced the original front cover illustrations with images from the Netflix series, making the link between the two works even more explicit. Although it is possible to watch the adaptation without reading the books and vice versa, the series rewards engagement across media through its complex narration. In this way, the series may be related to Jenkins's concept of transmedia storytelling since the story develops through interaction between different media versions, each making its unique contribution to the complex serial story.

Beyond *The End*

On January 1, 2019, Netflix released the last episode of *A Series of Unfortunate Events*, "The End." The episode illustrated the development of the series toward transmedial complexity as it developed beyond the plot in the book series. It begins with the introduction of a new character, a young girl who is searching for Lemony Snicket. He has, at this point, lost his authority as the narrator, having lost track of the Baudelaires. The girl's name is revealed to be Beatrice Baudelaire, indicating a relationship to the protagonists. Notably, the name "Beatrice" is connected to a paratextual mystery in the book series, as Snicket dedicates all of the novels to one beloved but long-dead and otherwise unidentified "Beatrice." However, the events in the final episode take place after Snicket's narration has ended and after he has written the dedications stating that this Beatrice is dead; therefore, she cannot be the girl in "The End," who instead appears to be Snicket's niece, Beatrice Baudelaire II. In the novel, Snicket's sister Kit washes up pregnant at an island, where the Baudelaire orphans have also been stranded. Kit is poisoned and dies giving birth; the orphans take charge of her infant daughter, marking their final development into independent caretakers rather than children to be cared for. They name the child after their mother, the last line in the book revealing that name to be "Beatrice"—and, therefore, also revealing that Snicket's long-lost love was the Baudelaire children's dead mother.

However, while the second Beatrice remains an infant in the book, the adaptation presents her at the age of about 10, on her own and searching for her uncle. This twist reveals how the adaptation moves beyond the events presented in *The End* by drawing on other source texts—especially the spin-off book *The Beatrice Letters*, which contains letters written by Lemony Snicket to the first Beatrice and by the second Beatrice to Snicket. Published in 2006, before the publication of *The End*, *The Beatrice Letters* does not reveal the identity of either Beatrice, and the fate of the Baudelaires remains uncertain in both books. However, by combining information revealed in *The End* and *The Beatrice Letters*, "The End" of the television series provides more closure than either of them. Thus, in the last scene in the episode, young Beatrice finally gets to meet her uncle, and the television series ends as she begins to tell him about the continuing adventures of the Baudelaire orphans. This final scene illustrates the series' development across media. By moving beyond *The End*, the ending of the adaptation presents a "unique contribution," in the words of Jenkins, to the ongoing development of the story. It complicates the relationship between the adaptation and the original as well as that between a child and an adult. That is, the ending illustrates the reversal of the roles of adults and children that is thematized throughout the series: The adult narrator has lost control of the story.[44] Moreover, he is turned into a listener, as Beatrice begins to tell him the continuing story of the Baudelaire children.

Notably, many fans complained that the ending of the television series provided too much closure or that it betrayed the book series by providing the "happy ending" that the books deny us. The critics argue that by providing answers to many of the questions that were left unanswered in the books, the adaptation departs from the central idea in the series of empowering the child readers by leaving it to them to find the answers and discuss the fate of the Baudelaires.[45] However, allowing the child Beatrice to take over the narration also appears to be a fitting ending to a series focusing on turning children into active and independent literary agents. Young Beatrice Baudelaire may thus represent the children who have engaged in the series over the years, even, like her, providing their own continuations.[46]

The difference between the two endings may also be considered in relation to the different conventions of literature and television series: The book series' lack of a happy ending undercuts the conventions of children's literature, but in television, open endings are more common since the logics of commercial television demand that series be continued until external factors such as decreasing popularity and budgetary issues put an end to them—as also reflected by the pausing of *The Familiar*, discussed in Chapter 2. Accordingly, the wrapped-up ending of the Netflix series in itself becomes controversial. Commenting on the decision to end the show after three seasons, actor Neil Patrick Harris (Count Olaf) emphasized the show's "finite" character: "I'm proud we're all doing something that's actually finite, and a piece of art. It's something that you can put on a bookshelf and appreciate for what it is, not just year after year hoping that people are still interested."[47] While the book series breaks with literary conventions by its lack of an ending, demonstrating that "the end is really the middle of the story," the television series becomes literary and "shelveable" by providing closure.

In the end, the differences between the book and television versions of *A Series of Unfortunate Events* reflect how the series is transformed across media. By providing closure, the adaptation presents itself as more than a repetition of the book series. In this way, it reflects a broader tendency wherein serial narratives are developed across media. The Snicket series uses its increasing narrative complexity to reverse the traditional power relations between children and adults within the story and beyond it while also complicating traditional hierarchical relations between literature and television, original and adaptation. In the following chapter, I continue to explore these narrative and transmedial dynamics in children's serial fiction, focusing on Philip Pullman's *His Dark Materials* and related materials.

Notes

1. An earlier version of this chapter first appeared in *Children's Literature Association Quarterly* 45, no. 1 (2020): 59–79. Copyright © 2020 Children's Literature Association.
2. Here, again, I refer to Mittell's concept of "shelveability," see Jason Mittell, *Complex TV. The Poetics of Contemporary Television Storytelling* (New York: New York University Press, 2015). All books are, of course, "shelveable," but the visual design of the Snicket series explicitly draws attention to this collectable aspect of the work, as was also the case with *The Familiar*. For further analysis of the collectability of the Snicket series, see Kendra Magnussen, "Lemony Snicket's *A Series of Unfortunate Events*: Daniel Handler and Marketing the Author," *Children's Literature Association Quarterly* 37, no. 1 (2012): 86–107.
3. Umberto Eco, *The Limits of Interpretation* (Bloomington and Indianapolis: Indiana University Press, 1990), 85.
4. Clarisse Loughrey, "A Series of Unfortunate Events Season 2 Review: Misery Makes a Welcome Return," *Independent,* March 30, 2018, www.independent.co.uk/arts-entertainment/tv/reviews/a-series-of-unfortunate-events-season-2-review-release-watch-netflix-date-cast-count-olaf-a8274776.html.
5. Sara Austin, "Performative Metafiction. Lemony Snicket, Daniel Handler and *The End* of *a Series of Unfortunate Events*," *The Looking Glass: New Perspectives on Children's Literature* 17, no. 1 (2013).
6. Eco, *Limits,* 88.
7. Bruce Butt, "'He's Behind You!' Reflections on Repetition and Predictability in Lemony Snicket's *a Series of Unfortunate* Events," *Children's Literature in Education* 34, no. 4 (2003): 282.
8. Ibid.
9. Frank Kelleter, "Five Ways of Looking at Popular Seriality," in *Media of Serial Narrative*, ed. Frank Kelleter (Columbus: The Ohio State University Press, 2017), 30.
10. Ibid. Original emphasis.
11. Ibid.
12. Ibid.
13. *A Series of Unfortunate Events: The Complete Wreck*, Harper Collins, October 13, 2006, www.harpercollins.ca/9780061119064/a-series-of-unfortunate-events-box-the-complete-wreck-books-1-13/.
14. Daniel Handler, "Fresh Air from WHYY," interview by Terry Gross, *NPR.org,* December 10, 2001, www.npr.org/templates/story/story.php?storyId=4212818.
15. I invoke the concept of narrative complexity, as presented Jason Mittell in relation to modern television series and introduced in Chapter 2 of this book. Mittell's concept is further discussed later in this chapter.
16. The cliff-hanger effect is stressed in the television adaptation, in "The Carnivorous Carnival—Part Two," as it marks the end of season 2, leaving the viewers uncertain about Klaus's and Violet's fates for an entire year.
17. Lemony Snicket, *The End* (New York: HarperCollins, 2006), 289.
18. For an interpretation of the narrator's voice, see Austin, "Metafiction."
19. Lemony Snicket, *The Wide Window* (New York: HarperCollins, 2000), 152.
20. Lemony Snicket, *The Reptile Room* (New York: HarperCollins, 1999), 123.
21. Ibid., 127.

22. Elizabeth Bullen, "Power of Darkness: Narrative and Biographical Reflexivity in *a Series of Unfortunate Events*," *International Research in Children's Literature* 1, no. 2 (2008): 11–12.
23. Austin, "Metafiction."
24. Magnussen, "Marketing," 88–89.
25. *A Series of Unfortunate Events*, season 1, episode 2, "The Bad Beginning—Part 2," developed by Mark Hudis and Barry Sonnenfeld (*Netflix*, 2017): 00:10–01:30.
26. My analysis is in accordance with recent developments within adaptation studies, moving away from an emphasis on the adaptation's fidelity toward the original, and focusing, instead, on the dynamic interaction between original and adaptation. See Linda Hutcheon, *A Theory of Adaptation* (New York: Routledge, 2006).
27. Loughrey, "Return."
28. Mittell, *Complex TV,* 53.
29. Ibid., 18. Original emphasis.
30. Ibid.
31. Henry Jenkins, "Transmedia Storytelling 101," *Confessions of an Aca-Fan*, March 21, 2007, http://henryjenkins.org/blog/2007/03/transmedia_storytelling_101.html.
32. Oriana Schwindt, "'A Series of Unfortunate Events' Renewed for Season Two at Netflix," *Variety,* March 13, 2017, https://variety.com/2017/tv/news/a-series-of-unfortunate-events-renewed-season-2-netflix-1202007658/.
33. Mittell, *Complex Tv,* 43.
34. Ibid., 43–44.
35. "Beginning—Part 2," 45:02.
36. *A Series of Unfortunate Events*, season 1, episode 3, "The Reptile Room—Part 1," developed by Mark Hudis and Barry Sonnenfeld (*Netflix*, 2017): 28:02–28:12.
37. *A Series of Unfortunate Events*, season 1, episode 8, "The Miserable Mill—Part 2," developed by Mark Hudis and Barry Sonnenfeld (*Netflix*, 2017): 29:41.
38. I refer to Mittell's concepts of narrative time in television, see Mittell, *Complex TV,* 26. "Story time" thus refers to the time frame of the diegesis, "discourse time" refers to the duration of the story as told within a given narrative, and "screen time"—or "narration time"—refers to the time it takes to consume the story.
39. Mittell, *Complex TV,* 51.
40. *A Series of Unfortunate Events*, season 1, episode 7, "The Miserable Mill — Part 1," developed by Mark Hudis and Barry Sonnenfeld (*Netflix*, 2017): 02:00–02:10.
41. For a detailed analysis of this scene, see Barbara Kaczyńska, "Metafiction in Children's Literature and its Adaptation on Screen. The Case of Lemony Snicket's A Series of Unfortunate Events," *New Horizons in English Studies* 3 (2018): 71–85.
42. Kaczyńska, "Metafiction," 83.
43. Linda Hutcheon, "Harry Potter and the Novice's Confession," *The Lion and the Unicorn* 32, no. 2 (2008): 175. Hutcheon here comments on Philip Pullman's *His Dark Materials* trilogy, which is analyzed in Chapter 4 of this book.
44. Snicket's loss of control is reflected in the fact that he does not know the whereabouts of his protagonists. This fact in itself marks a difference between the book

and the Netflix series since Snicket remains the narrator throughout book series, whereas the television series allows us to follow the events independently of his narration. Thus, while Snicket narrates the book version of *The End,* the adaptation presents him searching for the children, not knowing about the events on the island.

45. Marianne Eloise, "Here's Why a Series of Unfortunate Events' Ending Betray the Best Thing about the Books," *Digital Spy,* January 7, 2019, www.digitalspy.com/tv/a25773647/a-series-of-unfortunate-events-netflix-ending/.
46. The work's promotion of the child as an active actor may thus be considered in relation to the extensive production of fanfiction that surrounds the series. On online fora such as *FanFiction.net*, young readers publish their own stories related to the series, including continuations of the book series. In doing so, the children are literally overtaking the narration, illustrating the central theme in the series of turning children into active literary agents.
47. Morgan Jeffery, "Neil Patrick Harris Reveals Why a Series of Unfortunate Events Is Ending After Season 3," *Digital Spy,* March 29, 2018, www.digitalspy.com/tv/ustv/news/a853528/a-series-of-unfortunate-events-season-2-neil-patrick-harris-interview/.

4 Across Worlds and Volumes. Serial Space in Philip Pullman's *His Dark Materials*

Space is a central concept in the work of Philip Pullman. In his Patrick Hardy lecture, "Let's Write it in Red," Pullman associates children's books with "spaciousness": "Children's books open up out on a wideness and amplitude—a moral and mental spaciousness—that adult literature seems to have turned its back on."[1] The concept of "spaciousness" is associated with an openness toward other spaces; different mental and moral perspectives, as opposed to the fixed ideas and religious fanaticism that Pullman has dedicated most of his writing to oppose. In his works, the idea of spaciousness is developed through the concept of multiple worlds and the metaphor of the journey. Pullman's acclaimed trilogy *His Dark Materials* focuses on 11-year-old Lyra, who lives in a dimension parallel to the readers' world. Echoing the structure of the *bildungsroman*, the series follows Lyra's process of maturation as she leaves her home in her world's Victorianesque Oxford to travel into other dimensions. As the series progresses and Lyra crosses the boundaries between different worlds, and even between life and death, she moves toward the "mental and moral spaciousness" emphasized in the Hardy lecture. She gains knowledge and understanding of the worlds of others and her world through them. In this way, *His Dark Materials* illustrates an established idea of spatial dynamics in children's series literature, the concept of maturation through traveling.

This chapter traces how this concept is developed as Lyra's story is unfolded serially, both in the original trilogy and in related materials. Since its initial publication, Pullman's original trilogy has been supplemented by prequels and sequels, including the booklet *Lyra's Oxford* and a new trilogy, *The Book of Dust*, and it has been adapted into other media, for instance, in a recent HBO television adaptation. Focusing on this ongoing development of the series, the chapter continues the discussion of serialization as a transmedial process that was invoked in Chapter 3 in relation to *A Series of Unfortunate Events*. However, in this chapter, I specifically address the

DOI: 10.4324/9781003265894-4

relation between the serial format and the narrative representation of spaces and places in Pullman's work.

To connect the perspective of seriality with the spatial approach, I draw on the theory of storyworlds as developed by Marie-Laure Ryan, among others. A storyworld may be developed serially, even after the original story has ended, and the chapter accordingly traces how the Dark Materials storyworld is expanded as the story is developed serially, across volumes and media. The connection between the spatial and the serial aspect is motivated by an understanding of the series itself as a space to traverse. Thus, Lyra's journey into other worlds may be compared to the readers' journey into the serial storyworld. Like Lyra, readers gain an understanding of the expanding storyworld as they move through the series and the related materials, potentially moving toward maturation in the sense of a "mental and moral spaciousness" while they also, in many cases, literally grow up between the publication of each book. Thus, the concept of maturation through traveling both functions as a narrative scheme in the series and refers to the reader's experience of moving through the narrative space that is the series. I finally consider this process of serial maturation in relation to HBO's recent television adaption. The adaptation does not constitute an independent development of the story. However, by focusing on the concept of the storyworld, it becomes possible to consider how the adaption contributes to developing our view on Lyra's world by spatial exploration and how it, consequently, may lead to new forms of engagement with the series. The chapter thus contributes to the overall project of this book by exploring how the concept of the storyworld and a spatial approach to serial storytelling may lead to new insights into the relation between the narrative and medial aspects of serialization.

Space, Place, and Serial Storyworlds

Pullman's work and his concept of "spaciousness" in children's literature may be understood through the central concepts in space and place theory. The concept of "space," according to Yi-Fu Tuan's definition, implies an idea of freedom and openness, while the notion of "place" is associated with security. "'Space' is more abstract than 'place.' What begins as undifferentiated space becomes place as we get to know it better and endow it with value," Tuan claims, further noting that "if we think of space as that which allows movement, then place is pause; each pause in movement makes it possible for location to be transformed into place."[2] Tuan's primary example of a place, in the sense of a location endowed with personal value, is the home: "There is no place like home."[3] "Space," on the other hand, is associated with movement and openness. Contrasting with the safe place of the home, it may be related to the idea of traveling.

Tuan's concept of space may accordingly be related to the metaphorical "spaciousness" addressed by Pullman in the Hardy lecture and the metaphor of maturation through traveling. According to Peter Hunt, this metaphor is widespread in children's literature:

> The journey is a central, vital element of children's literature. In texts for "younger" readers, it is often a metaphor for exploration and education; readers go . . . in a circle that enables them to gain knowledge—possibly to be stabbed by experience—and to return to home and security, and to get a satisfying psychological closure.[4]

Hunt describes the structure of the *bildungsroman*: The protagonist matures by moving away from the safe place of the childhood home and traveling into unknown spaces. Notably, according to Hunt, the metaphor also applies to the reading experience.[5] The reader travels with the protagonist into the space of the story and then returns "home" to safety and closure. He notes how this metaphor becomes strong in relation to fantasy fiction and quotes Ursula K. LeGuin, who states that "fantasy is a journey . . . into the subconscious mind."[6] Thus, the narrative scheme of maturation through traveling may be related to the concept of reading as a journey into the imagination.

From a narratological perspective, Marie-Laure Ryan also notes this connection. She focuses on the metaphor "life is a journey," which underlies the maturation through traveling scheme, and observes, "On a meta-narrative level, the blending of two common metaphors, 'life is a story' and 'life is a journey' produces a widespread spatial conceptualization of 'narrative is a journey.'"[7] The metaphor of the journey thus illustrates a spatial approach to narrative, which is otherwise primarily associated with temporality. Ryan combines narrative theory with space and place theory to provide the tools to analyze this spatial dimension. In *Narrating Space/Spatializing Narrative*, she and her fellow editors distinguish between the representation of space in narratives at different levels.[8] Apart from the "story space" and the "setting," which covers all of the places where the story takes place, they invoke the concept of the "storyworld," which they define as "the story space completed by the reader's imagination on the basis of the principle of minimal departure."[9] The "principle of minimal departure" is "a principle that urges readers to build their mental representation of fictional worlds on the basis of their life experience and knowledge of the world, as long as this knowledge is not contradicted by the text."[10] The concept becomes relevant in relation to Pullman's trilogy because Pullman operates with multiple dimensions. Lyra's dimension is similar yet different from the real world as known by the readers. To imagine her world, readers must combine their knowledge of the real world with knowledge about the storyworld that the work provides. Ryan et al. note, "In a story that refers to both real and imaginary locations, the storyworld superimposes the locations specific to the text onto the geography of the actual world."[11]

The emphasis on storyworlds marks a spatial turn in narrative theory. While traditional narratology focuses on "narrative" in the sense of a succession of events, this new tendency implies an emphasis on the spaces or "worlds" where the story takes place. Ryan notes that "a storyworld is more than a static container for the objects mentioned in a story; it is a dynamic model of evolving situations, and its representation in the recipient's mind is a simulation of the changes that are caused by the events of the plot."[12] Thus, the concept may not be reduced to a static map of the places where the story takes place but refers to the continuous development of these places as the story unfolds across volumes and media. "Nowadays we have not only multimodal representations of storyworlds," writes Ryan, "but also serial storyworlds that span multiple installments and transmedial storyworlds that are deployed simultaneously across multiple media platforms, resulting in a media landscape in which creators and fans alike constantly expand, revise, and even parody them."[13] A storyworld may be expanded serially, even after the original story has ended, as is indeed the case with Pullman's series, and this development may, in turn, influence modes of engaging with the series.[14] The concept of storyworlds thus makes it possible to connect a spatial approach to narrative with the perspectives of seriality and transmediality. The remaining part of this chapter explores how the *Dark Materials* storyworld is expanded serially across volumes and media in ways that contribute to developing the maturation-through-traveling metaphor, beginning with the original trilogy, *The Golden Compass, The Subtle Knife,* and *The Amber Spyglass.*

His Dark Materials—The Original Trilogy

"Lyra and her dæmon moved through the darkening hall, taking care to keep to one side, out of the sight of the kitchen."[15] The opening lines in the trilogy's volume 1, *The Golden Compass*, introduces the protagonist Lyra by locating her in space. The first words, "Lyra and her dæmon," hint that the story is set in another world. Everybody in Lyra's world has a dæmon who represents their personality or soul in the shape of an animal, and while the reader may not know this, the word "dæmon," invoked without explanation, already suggests an otherworldly setting. The sentence furthermore emphasizes movement: Lyra and her dæmon are moving through a "darkening hall." The hall is a space of passage. Lyra and her dæmon are on their way to enter a forbidden space, the Retiring Room, where the events will occur that lead to the onset of the story and of Lyra's journey.

From the outset, Lyra is thus presented in movement. The trilogy is hereafter structured by her journey. *The Golden Compass* focuses on Lyra's departure from her home at Jordan College in Oxford. She travels first to London with her later-to-be-revealed mother, Mrs. Coulter, and then to the undefined territory of the North. The volume functions as an introduction to the logics and creatures of Lyra's world and concludes as she leaves this world by using the bridge which her father, Lord Asriel, has created to reach other dimensions. The second volume, *The Subtle Knife*, opens in a world that is a fictional version of the readers' world and follows the boy Will, who finds a portal to another world where he meets Lyra. The volume thus introduces the concept of multiple worlds and connects Lyra's world and her story to Will's and the readers' world. Volume 3, *The Amber Spyglass*, takes Lyra and Will's journey one step further as they move into numerous other worlds and even transgress metaphysical boundaries between life and death, visiting the world of the dead. They move on to find each other in the Eden-like world of the wheeled creatures, the Mulefas. In this way, the story spins outward as each volume reflects different steps in Lyra's journey and represents an expansion of the storyworld. The series culminates when Lyra falls in love with Will and experiences a sexual awakening, metaphorically entering into the worlds of the adults before she finally returns to Jordan College, completing the cycle of her journey.

At first glance, *His Dark Materials* relates to the concept of maturation through traveling, described by Hunt. However, as noted by Amanda Greenwell, Pullman complicates this idea. His transformation of the classic *bildungsroman* happens first and foremost through his presentation of Lyra's unconventional childhood home.[16] According to Perry Nodelman, "Home represents above all a place where change is unlikely or even impossible, a safely static enclosure designed to keep uncertainty and flux outside."[17] However, this idea of the home is far from describing Lyra's home at Jordan College. By placing Lyra within a university context, Pullman presents her home as a space for development rather than static enclosure. Since Lyra's world is characterized by Victorian social norms and gender roles, for Lyra, as a female child, Jordan College becomes a space to transgress, as suggested by the opening lines that present her as she sneaks into the forbidden room. Her controversial position is stressed in the description of her life at the college:

> What she liked best was clambering over the College roofs with Roger, the kitchen boy . . . to spit plumstones on the heads of passing Scholars . . . or waging war. Just as she was unaware of the hidden currents

of politics running below the surface of College affairs, so the Scholars, for their part, would have been unable to see the rich seething stew of alliances and enmities and feuds and treaties which was a child's life in Oxford.[18]

Climbing on roofs and playing with servants, Lyra transgresses the college's social norms and physical boundaries. Her childhood's Oxford is presented as a separate world from that of the adults. Pullman thus introduces the concept of multiple worlds long before introducing the idea of multiple dimensions. Children and adults live in the same place yet in different social spaces—as emphasized in the contrast between the adult's view of the children's play as "innocent and charming" with the child's experience of real war.

This emphasis on contrasting worlds is stressed in the series as Pullman moves on to explore the idea of multiple dimensions. The depiction of Lyra's Jordan as an unconventional home space is stressed by the representation of Oxford as an *unheimlich*—unhomely—otherworldly place. Most readers will know the city, but Pullman disturbs this sense of familiarity as it becomes clear that Lyra's Oxford is different from the real city. For instance, Jordan College does not exist in the real world. Pullman thus destabilizes the relation between the real-life place and the fictional space through the concept of multiple worlds, "opening up" real-life places with the abstract potentiality of other worlds. The resulting experience of defamiliarization is reflected in Lyra's reaction when she arrives in the Oxford of Will's and the readers' world in *The Subtle Knife*. "This is a different Oxford,"[19] she exclaims, shocked. Will is surprised by her helplessness: "He couldn't know how much of her childhood had been spent running about streets almost identical with these, and how proud she'd been of belonging to Jordan College . . . and now it simply wasn't there, and she wasn't Lyra of Jordan anymore; she was a lost little girl in a strange world."[20] Here, the significance of Jordan for Lyra's identity is emphasized: the place defines her, and without it, she is lost.

Lyra's experience of the other world echoes the readers' confrontation with her world in the first volume. Sarah Cantrell argues that "*The Subtle Knife* deliberately thwarts readers' acclimation to the world of *The Golden Compass* by asking them to view their world through Lyra's uncomprehending gaze. If Pullman's readers are to make sense of difference, they must reflect on how they appear in the eyes of another."[21] The serial experience of reading first *The Golden Compass* and then *The Subtle Knife* means that readers are made to see their world from the outside. This confrontation with the other world arguably marks one step toward maturation for Lyra and the readers. That is, while Lyra initially feels lost in Will's Oxford, her entrance into his world also marks her increasing understanding of the world—hers and the world of others. She seeks out the scientist Mary Malone, who tells her about her research into dark matter, and Lyra learns about matters that were kept from her in her world. As she enters Malone's office building, Lyra feels better, expressed in the sentence "This was like home again,"[22] which suggests that the feeling of "home" is related to the space of knowledge rather than to Jordan, specifically.

Lyra's journey culminates in *The Amber Spyglass*, where she falls in love with Will. The emphasis on maturation, in the sense of increasing knowledge, is here related to maturation in the sense of sexual awakening. This experience is described metaphorically in terms of a homecoming. "Lyra felt something strange happen to her body. . . . She felt as if she had been handed the key to a giant house she hadn't known was there, a house that was somehow inside her, and as she turned the key, deep in the darkness of the building she felt other doors opening too, and lights coming on."[23] Greenwell notes how the idea of maturation as homecoming reflects the idea of the home in Pullman's work, which she summarizes as follows. "True home is not simply the protective and often limiting place to which one might return after an adventure, but a vibrant, dynamic space that functions as an integral component to thoughtful and active participation in the world."[24]

Greenwell's insight into Pullman's remodeling of the home contributes to an understanding of the maturation-through-traveling scheme. Lyra does mature as she travels; however, her journey does not lead away from the home. Rather, she moves from a relation to the home characterized by transgression toward a homecoming within herself. The centrality of homecoming in the series is reflected in the ending of the trilogy, as Lyra and Will have to separate and go home to their respective worlds. The windows between the worlds are closed, and the story literally concludes with closure. Upon separating, the children agree to sit once a year on the same bench in the botanical garden in Oxford in each of their worlds. Lyra suggests, "if we could come here at the same time . . . then we could pretend we were close again—because we *would* be close, if you sat here and I sat just *here* in my world."[25] This idea, to be close at the same place, "here," yet in different worlds, reflects how Pullman uses the concept of multiple worlds to complicate the relation between the specific place, "here," and the imaginary spaces of other worlds and people. Lyra and Will pretend to be together, using their imagination. Thus, the imagination is presented as the gateway to other worlds and the "mental and moral spaciousness" invoked in the Hardy lecture—an idea which becomes central as Lyra's story continues with the Book of Dust series.

Returning to Fantasy: *Lyra's Oxford* and the Book of Dust

The ending of the Dark Materials trilogy did not point toward a continuation. On the contrary, Pullman stressed the necessity of homecoming and closure. Yet, he did return to Lyra's world, first in two small books, *Once Upon a Time in the North* and *Lyra's Oxford*. The latter is of particular interest to this study as it contains the story "Lyra and the Birds," focusing on 15-year-old Lyra and her developing relation to her home in Oxford.

The first sentence in "Lyra and the Birds" indicates Lyra's new relation to her home: "Lyra didn't often climb out of her bedroom window these days. She had a better way on to the roof of Jordan College: the Porter had given her a key that let her on to the roof of the Lodge Tower."[26] Lyra no longer transgresses the borders of the college. She has a key, which indicates that she is now in control and truly at home. The key recalls the key that was evoked when her sexual awakening was described in *The Amber Spyglass*: "She felt that she had been handed the key to a giant house."[27] Jordan College is, indeed, a giant house, and Lyra's process of maturation is thus reflected in her relation to the physical space of her home. "Lyra and the Birds" describes how Lyra is lured by a witch, who is trying to get her killed, but she is saved as the birds of Oxford warn her. The story ends as Lyra reflects on the birds' protection as a manifestation of the city, thinking: "The city, their city—*belonging* was one of the meanings of that, and *protection*, and *home*."[28]

This significance of the childhood home is stressed in *La Belle Sauvage* (2017), volume 1 in Pullman's new series *Book of Dust*. A prequel to the original Dark Materials trilogy, *La Belle Sauvage* describes how the infant Lyra was brought to Jordan by the boy Malcolm Polstead, who rescues her from a rainstorm and brings her down a river in his canoe. He eventually manages to reach Asriel, her father, who places the infant in the care of the Jordan Collage. In this way, Jordan's significance in *Lyra's Oxford*, as a place, in the sense of Tuan, associated with belonging and protection, is explained: The walls of the collage literally protect Lyra from the people who have wanted to get to her since she was born.

This emphasis on the home in *Lyra's Oxford* and *La Belle Sauvage* may be opposed to the emphasis on traveling in the original trilogy. Rather than expanding the storyworld, the function is first and foremost to allow readers to return "home" to the now-familiar world of *His Dark Materials*. According to Umberto Eco, this idea of returning to the familiar universe is one of the central motivations for consuming serial narratives. He notes that "with a series one believes one is enjoying the novelty of the story (which is always the same) while in fact one is enjoying it because of the recurrence of a narrative scheme that remains constant."[29] *Lyra's Oxford* and *La Belle*

Sauvage do emphasize the idea of returning to a familiar universe. However, they do so not by repeating the story but by allowing readers to get a new, expanded view of Lyra's world in Oxford. Accordingly, the serial development in Lyra's story beyond the original trilogy may best be described by the use of Ryan's concept of serial storyworlds, as described earlier. Notably, Ryan emphasizes the participatory aspects of storyworlds, as "creators and fans alike constantly expand, revise and even parody them."[30] *Lyra's Oxford*, in particular, seems to promote such participatory engagement. For instance, the book includes a map of Lyra's Oxford which encourages readers to compare the fictional city to the real Oxford, an activity which is often carried out by readers who visits Oxford as a form of literary tourism.[31] The book furthermore includes several visual representations of things: Postcards, a list of books, a brochure, the inclusion of which first of all points to the spatial—visual and material—dimension of the book. These things are seemingly not related to the story in the book, but, as Pullman notes in the foreword, they might make sense in relation to the future developments of the series, and the reader is thus encouraged to actively trace connections and piece the story together across volumes.

This activity becomes specifically relevant in relation to the second volume in the *Book of Dust* series, *The Secret Commonwealth*. Several characters and things presented in the previous works gain new significance in this story, and their parts in the bigger plot become visible. For instance, the alchemist Sebastian Makepeace, whom Lyra meets in "Lyra and the Birds," becomes a significant link to the titular "secret commonwealth" in the new book, and Malcolm Polstead, the boy protagonist in *La Belle Sauvage* (who is also Lyra's professor in "Lyra and the Birds") grows into character as the male hero of the story. Furthermore, several of the things that appear in *Lyra's Oxford* reappear in *The Secret Commonwealth*. For instance, Lyra finds a brochure for the ferry S.S. Zenobia, which also appears as a visual document in *Lyra's Oxford*.

In his foreword to *The Secret Commonwealth*, Pullman stresses the serial relation between this book and his previous works. He notes,

> events have consequences, and sometimes the effects of what we once did take a long time to become fully apparent. At the same time, the world moves on; power and influences shift, or increase, or diminish; and the problems and concerns of adult people are not necessarily the same as the ones they had when young. Lyra and Malcolm . . . are not children any more.

The events in *The Secret Commonwealth* have presented consequences of what happened in *His Dark Materials* and *La Belle Sauvage*. The books are thus presented as parts of the same story, yet the perspective changes. The story focuses on Lyra as an adult, and this change of perspective arguably contributes to the development of the storyworld and its relation to the real world, as perceived by the readers.

The story begins as Lyra, now 20 years old, is estranged from her childhood home in Jordan. The college has a new master, who asks her to leave the rooms where she lived as a child. He motivates the decision by presenting Jordan College as a gendered male space. "You see, the rooms on that staircase are really needed for undergraduates, for our young men."[32] Lyra's transgression of the social norms is no longer accepted, a situation which is stressed by the fact that political forces are working to repeal the law of academic sanctuary, which has kept her safe at Jordan. Lyra finds herself homeless, a condition which is stressed by her internal state as she is in disagreement with her dæmon, Pantalaimon. Their complex relation is indicated in the opening lines of the novel:

> Pantalaimon, the dæmon of Lyra Belacqua, now called Lyra Silvertongue, lay along the window sill [sic] of Lyra's little study-bedroom in St Sophia's College in a state as far from thought as he could get. He was aware of the cold draught from the ill-fitting sash window beside him, and of the warm naphtha light on the desk below the window, and of the scratching of Lyra's pen, and of the darkness outside. It was the cold and the dark he most wanted just then.[33]

The story opens with the dæmon's perspective, as opposed to the opening in *His Dark Materials*, "Lyra and her dæmon."[34] Back then, they were one. Now, Pantalaimon is lying in the window, in a passage between Lyra and the warmth inside and the cold outside. The opening reflects Lyra's internal division; her dæmon does not want to share a space with her. Their disagreement is due to Lyra's obsession with popular theories of rationalism and relativism, which claim, respectively, that "it was nothing more than what it was"[35] and that nothing means more than anything else. Pantalaimon opposes these theories, which include visions of a world without dæmons, and he argues that they contradict everything he and Lyra learned on their previous journey: "The other worlds. The subtle knife. The witches. There's no room for them in the universe you want to believe in."[36] According to the dæmon, Lyra's new mentors reduce the world to "what there is"; they leave no space for the imagination. Thus, they exclude the part of the human being that is represented by the dæmons and which allows them to imagine the possible, the other worlds.

Pantalaimon finally leaves Lyra. When she wakes up to find that he is gone, she finds a note: "GONE TO LOOK FOR YOUR IMAGINATION."[37] Lyra is thus left in an uncanny, *unheimlich*, state, as a person without a dæmon, and the novel follows her journey to find him. Again, she moves into unknown territories, this time going South and East. While this journey does not go across dimensions, it does bring her into contact with other worlds, including the titular "secret commonwealth," which is "a world of hidden things and hidden relationships. It's the reason that nothing is only itself."[38] Confronted with this world, Lyra begins to question her rationalist ideas.

> If rationality can't see things like the secret commonwealth, it's because rationality's vision is limited. The secret commonwealth is *there*. We can't see it with rationality any more than we can weigh something with a microscope: it's the wrong sort of instrument. We need to imagine as well as measure.[39]

Lyra's maturation in *The Secret Commonwealth* is associated with this realization that "we need to imagine as well as measure." She has this realization while she is on a ferry, on her way to the Middle East. The ferry soon after hits a boat, which is filled with refugees, and Lyra is thrown into the chaos of the Middle Eastern crisis. Her journey thus brings her into contact with events that reflect the refugee crises in Europe at the time of the book's publication in 2019. This hint to real-world politics suggests that the imaginary world should be seen not as an escape into fantasy but as a way to see reality through the lens of the imagination. Pullman resists the categorization of his books as fantasy fiction; they are, he argues, "stark realism."[40] He only uses "the fantastical elements to say something that I thought was true about us and about our lives."[41] *The Secret Commonwealth* thus expands the Dark Materials storyworld by emphasizing the connection between our world and Lyra's. Like Lyra, the readers travel into another world in order to gain a better understanding of the real world. Maturation, according to Pullman, is to travel into the unknown spaces of the imagination *and* return home to the real world—to imagine and to measure.

The *Book of Dust* series has not yet reached its ending, as I am writing this in 2021. The backdrop of doing serial criticism is the condition of writing about still unfinished stories. However, following Ryan, the idea of focusing on storyworlds is to be able to capture the dynamic of continuously developing and expanding stories. Accordingly, it makes sense to move on to examine Pullman's storyworld, as it is developed across media, in HBO's 2019 television adaptation.

Returning to Jordan—now on HBO

HBO's television adaptation of *His Dark Materials* opens dramatically one stormy night, with a man knocking on the door of Jordan College. The man is Lord Asriel, and in his arms is an infant, Lyra. The door is opened by the dean of the college, and Asriel trusts him with the baby, invoking the law of academic sanctuary. Hereafter, the series moves forward to 11-year-old Lyra and her life in Jordan, recalling the first chapter of the book series. However, the opening scene with Asriel in the storm reflects how the adaptation relies not only on the original trilogy but also on the related material: The circumstances of how Lyra got to Jordan is described in full detail only in *La Belle Sauvage*, published two years prior to the release of the HBO series' first season in 2019. By including this later added prehistory, the television series presents itself not merely as an adaptation of a specific book but rather of the whole story as it has been developed across volumes and media.

The HBO series first aired in November 2019. Its release followed quickly after the publication of Pullman's long-expected continuation of Lyra's story in *The Secret Commonwealth*, thus profiting from the renewed interest in the Dark Materials storyworld (and vice versa). The series is far from the only adaptation. Most famously, a film adaptation of *The Golden Compass* premiered in 2007 but failed in terms of both critical acclaim and sales of theater tickets. It was never followed by adaptations of volumes 2 and 3. Many opinions have been expressed about why and how the film failed. While this essay is not the place to repeat or unfold them, it is worth mentioning that the format of the television series may be better suited than the shorter film format to present the complex story. Thus, while the film presented the entire plot of volume 1 in 113 minutes, the HBO series spent its whole first season, eight episodes, to represent the same story. This format allowed the series to represent the storyworld in more detail, including scenes from the related materials, such as the scene with Asriel in the storm, and the succeeding volumes in the trilogy. From the beginning, the television series thus presents the story about Lyra's first adventures in the North within a larger context, with hints to Lyra's past as well as her future.

Furthermore, the television series is able to focus more on representing places and developing the storyworld. For instance, the first episode is titled "Lyra's Jordan" and presents Lyra's childhood as she is climbing on roofs and moving around in the recognizable yet otherworldly city of Oxford. The series is filmed in the iconic city and dwells at the monumental university buildings, thus stressing the already strong link in the story to the historical atmosphere of the city. Lyra's life of transgression and play in this fictional Oxford is contrasted with her life later, in Mrs. Coulter's London apartment, which is depicted as a fashionable, but strictly limited space, where escape seems impossible since the elevator opens directly into the apartment. This place is again contrasted with Lyra's life after she escapes the apartment, living among the gypsies on the river and later in a frozen and deserted arctic landscape of the North. While the events are all present in the movie, the television series has time to dwell on the visual representation of these different places and worlds that they represent and, thus, expose the contrasts between them.

The contrasts between different places and worlds become even more explicit as the series begins to juxtapose scenes and events happing in the different volumes—and thus in different worlds. From episode 4 and onward, Lyra's story, as presented in *The Golden Compass*, is mixed with scenes from *The Subtle Knife;* that is, scenes that take place in the real world and involve the second protagonist Will. Lyra's journey to the North is contrasted with Will's modern everyday life in an English town. The contrast culminates in the final episode, where the perspective shifts rapidly between Lyra's world and Will's. Lyra is situated on a frozen mountain where she is trying to prevent her father, Asriel, from separating her friend Roger from his dæmon, using the energy from this separation (which eventually kills Roger) to create a bridge to another world. Will, on the other hand, is located in summery Oxford, trying to escape the police. During his escape, he finds a window to another world, and the series' first season ends as he climbs through the window, while Lyra, simultaneously it appears, crosses the bridge created by her father.

The effect of this juxtaposition of events from different volumes is that the viewers are presented to the concept of multiple worlds much earlier than in the book series: In the latter, readers spend the entire first volume getting familiar with the logics of Lyra's world, only to be—somewhat shockingly—thrown back to the real world in the opening of volume 2, where Will is first introduced. The adaptation, in contrast, from the beginning presents Lyra's journey to the North within the bigger context of the series, hinting at the future developments of the story and the idea of multiple worlds, while also invoking the prehistory about Lyra's infancy, as suggested by the opening scene. The different media may partly explain this difference: The television series does not need as much time as the books to introduce the viewers to Lyra's world: How it looks and sounds and which features distinguishes it from our world, and it may thus move on to shifting between this world and Will's without confusing the audience. However, the difference can also be explained by the serial relation between the two works: As an adaptation of a well-known children's book series, the television series may assume that many viewers will already be experienced with the storyworld and with the multiple world logics of *His Dark Materials*.

In Chapter 3 of this book, I already commented on this idea in relation to the serial development of Snicket's *A Series of Unfortunate Events:* the idea that readers grow up and become more experienced as a series progresses across volumes and media. I invoked Linda Hutcheon's observation that "readers literally go from innocence to experience over the course of a narrative, and certainly in moving from an adapted text to an adaptation, they become 'knowing' readers, no longer presumed innocent."[42] Hutcheon here, specifically, reflects on *His Dark Materials*. She evokes Lyra's development from innocence to experience in the series, suggesting that the ideal reader undergoes a similar transformation as the series progresses. This becomes evident already in the original trilogy in the contrast between *The Golden Compass*, which presents a rather straightforward adventure, Lyra's fight against evil child abductors, and *The Amber Spyglass*, which relates the story to a complex philosophical discussion of morality, sexual awakening, and the fall of man, and with multiple quotes by William Blake and John Milton. Thus, similarly to the Snicket book series, *His Dark Materials* confronts its readers with gradually more complex material, seemingly addressing a more mature reader as the series progresses.

Notably, *His Dark Materials*, like most children's books, can be read at different levels: Hutcheon notes how most children's series address both children and adults, including the adults reading for or with the children, and the adults whom the children grow up to be as they read, or in-between volumes or versions.[43] This temporal aspect becomes specifically relevant in relation to *His Dark Materials*, which has been developed over more than 20 years, from the publication of *The Golden Compass* in 1995 to *The Secret Commonwealth* and the television adaptation in 2019, both of which appear to be targeted at a more mature (if still young) audience. In *The Secret Commonwealth*, Lyra is 20 years old, and, as stressed by Pullman in the foreword, her problems, ranging from the loss of her dæmon to her love life, reflect her age, which she may share with the readers who have matured with her. Similarly, the television series is not marketed as a children's series but is targeted toward HBO's adult audience, reflecting the assumption that many viewers will be adults, who read the book series as children in the 1990s, when it was first published.

In the sense that viewers, or readers, are returning to the storyworld after a long time, the experience of watching the adaption may be considered in terms of a homecoming. Thus, while the original trilogy spins outward, confronting the reader with still more worlds and complex matters of religion and philosophy, the television adaptation, like *Lyra's Oxford*, focuses on producing recognition, allowing viewers to return "home" to Lyra's Oxford and the original story. However, as discussed earlier, the concept of the home is complicated in *His Dark Materials* as it is associated with maturation: When Lyra comes home, she is not the same after her journey, and the adaptation, similarly, is not the same as the original series; it is not a mere repetition of the plot in *The Golden Compass* but re-structures and complicates the story. Viewers who have read the trilogy and other books will be able to acknowledge how the adaptation contributes to developing the storyworld and, not least, its relation to the real world. Accordingly, the question of the readers' maturation is a question not only about age but also about how the readers gradually become "knowing" and experienced with the storyworld as it is developed across volumes and media.

Conclusion

Lyra's story is not complete as I am writing this in 2021. We do not know how her journey will end, but we do know where she is going. She has dreamt of a red building, which recalls the house invoked in *The Amber Spyglass*, the "house that was somehow inside her."[44] *The Secret Commonwealth* ends as she travels to find this house. It ends with an open "to be concluded."[45] Lyra and the readers are still moving into the unknown spaces of the expanding storyworld; yet they are also moving toward this specific place and, possibly, toward a homecoming.

This process of navigating between unknown spaces and familiar places may be related to the concept of serial complexity and the dynamic of moving between recognition or repetition and variation, discussed in the previous chapters of this book. Like *The Familiar*, Pullman's work builds familiarity as the series progresses, and readers become increasingly knowing of Lyra's world. And like *A Series of Unfortunate Events*, Pullman's series also confronts readers with increasing narrative complexity as the storyworld is expanded across volumes and media, including more dimensions and addressing an increasingly mature audience. This chapter, specifically, has contributed to developing the concept of serial maturation, focusing on the spatial metaphor of maturation through traveling in *His Dark Materials* and relating to both Lyra's development and the serial reading experience. Lyra matures as she travels into unknown spaces, associated with openness and possibility—and as she returns home to see familiar places with new eyes.

Similarly, readers of the series are confronted with other worlds as they travel across the space that is the serial storyworld. First, they are confronted with Lyra's world in *The Golden Compass*; then, they see their world through Lyra's gaze in *The Subtle Knife*. Finally, in *The Amber Spyglass*, the windows between the worlds are closed, and readers, as well as Lyra, must return to reality. Maturation, here, is associated with homecoming because "there is no elsewhere."[46] The development of the story beyond the trilogy further complicates the maturation-through-traveling scheme. *Lyra's Oxford* and *The Book of Dust* develop Lyra's relation with her home. Rather than traveling away from childhood, Lyra needs to find her way back to her childhood imagination. Notably, these books and the television series also mark a return for the readers to the world of *His Dark Materials*, that is, to the world of children's literature. Pullman's return to Lyra's world may be read as an attempt to reach those adult readers who have, like Lyra, gotten lost in the idea that "there is nothing more than what there is."

Maturation, in *His Dark Materials*, is thus not presented simply as a journey from childhood to adulthood but is associated with a development toward the "mental and moral spaciousness" that Pullman evokes in his Patrick Hardy lecture. It is the ability to imagine other worlds and navigate between the potentiality of space and the reality of place, as captured by the metaphors of the journey and the home. While Lyra, the child, in *His Dark Materials*, has to return to her world because "there is no elsewhere," adult Lyra, in *The Secret Commonwealth*, has to find her imagination because "there is always more than what there is." For the readers, this "more" may be found by traveling through the expanding serial storyworld of His Dark Materials.

Notes

1. Philip Pullman, "Let's Write It in Red. The Patrick Hardy Lecture," *Signal*, no. 85 (1998): 44.
2. Yi-Fu Tuan, *Space and Place: The Perspective of Experience* (Minneapolis: University of Minnesota Press, 1977), 6.
3. Ibid., 3.
4. Peter Hunt, "Landscapes and Journeys, Metaphors and Maps: The Distinctive Feature of English Fantasy," *Children's Literature Association Quarterly* 12, no. 1 (1987): 11.
5. Ibid.
6. Quoted in Ibid.
7. Marie-Laure Ryan, "Space," in *The Living Handbook of Narratology*, eds. Peter Hühn et al. (Hamburg: Hamburg University, 2012), www.lhn.uni-hamburg.de/node/55.html.
8. Marie-Laure Ryan, Kenneth Foote and Maoz Azaryahu, *Narrating Space/Spatializing Narrative. Where Narrative Theory and Geography Meet* (Columbus: The Ohio State University Press, 2016).
9. Ibid., 24.
10. Ibid., 20.
11. Ibid., 24.
12. Marie-Laure Ryan, "Story/World/Media. Turning the Instruments of a Media-Conscious Narratology," in *Storyworlds Across Media. Toward a Media-Conscious Narratology*, eds. Marie-Laure Ryan and Jan-Noël Thon (Lincoln and London: University of Nebraska Press, 2014), 33.
13. Marie-Laure Ryan and Jan-Noël Thon, eds., *Storyworlds Across Media. Toward a Media-Conscious Narratology* (Lincoln and London: University of Nebraska Press, 2014), 1.
14. For more on the aspect of engagement, see Susana Tosca and Lisbeth Klastrup, *Transmedial Worlds in Everyday Life* (New York: Routledge, 2019).

15. Philip Pullman, *His Dark Materials* (London: Scholastic, 2012), 9.
16. Amanda M. Greenwell, "Remodeling Home in Philip Pullman's *His Dark Materials*," *The Lion and the Unicorn* (January 2018): 20–36.
17. Perry Nodelman, *The Hidden Adult: Defining Children's Literature* (Baltimore: Johns Hopkins University Press, 2008), 66.
18. Pullman, *Dark Materials*, 35.
19. Ibid., 386.
20. Ibid.
21. Sarah K. Cantrell, "Nothing Like Pretend. Difference, Disorder and Dystopia in the Multiple World Spaces of Philip Pullman's His Dark Materials," *Children's Literature in Education* 41 (2010): 313.
22. Pullman, *Dark Materials*, 396.
23. Ibid., 953.
24. Greenwell, "Remodeling," 21.
25. Pullman, *Dark Materials*, 1007.
26. Philip Pullman, *Lyra's Oxford* (New York: Doubleday, Penguin Random House, 2017), 3.
27. Pullman, *Dark Materials*, 953.
28. Pullman, *Lyra's Oxford*, 47.
29. Umberto Eco, *The Limits of Interpretation* (Bloomington: Indiana University Press, 1990), 86.
30. Ryan and Thon, eds., *Storyworlds Across Media*, 1.
31. Maria Sachiko Cecire, Hannah Field, Kavita Mundan Finn and Malini Roy, eds., *Space and Place in Children's Literature, 1789 to the Present* (New York: Routledge, 2016), 12.
32. Philip Pullman, *The Secret Commonwealth* (London: Penguin Books LTD, 2019), 96.
33. Ibid., 1.
34. Pullman, *Dark Materials*, 9.
35. Ibid., 76.
36. Ibid., 191.
37. Ibid., 194.
38. Ibid., 427.
39. Ibid., 482.
40. Philip Pullman, "Questions and Answers," *Philip Pullman* (website), 2009, www.philip-pullman.com/qas?searchtext=&page=5.
41. Ibid.
42. Linda Hutcheon, "Harry Potter and the Novice's Confession," *The Lion and the Unicorn* 32, no. 2 (2008): 175.
43. Ibid.
44. Pullman, *Commonwealth*, 953.
45. Ibid., 687.
46. Pullman, *Dark Materials*, 1007.

5 Keep listening!
Born-Audio Serials and Serialization as a Business Model

In 2016, the Swedish subscription service for audiobooks and e-books, Storytel, launched a new brand: Storytel Originals. Storytel Originals are serial narratives, typically in popular genres such as romance, science fiction, and crime fiction, and written specifically for the audiobook format. These "born-audio" texts exemplify how producers of literary content in new media contexts turn toward the feuilleton format that already dominated 19th-century popular fiction. Furthermore, Storytel's audiobook series reflect a clear inspiration from the world of television series, in relation to both content and narrative structure. They are presented in episodes and seasons, and the name of the brand resonates with the original brand of the streaming service for television series and film Netflix, Netflix Originals. This chapter will focus on the case of Storytel Originals as an example of the current resurgence of the serial format in literature: How contemporary literary producers, such as Storytel, make use of the serial format in ways that lend inspiration from other media and media cultures, while also developing the serial form and narrative content according to the affordances of the audiobook and the conditions of a digitalized book market.

The previous chapters of this book have provided examples of how the serial format migrates across media. In the case of Danielewski's *The Familiar*, discussed in Chapter 2, we saw how the narrative structure of television series inspired the printed novel. Chapters 3 and 4 demonstrate how television series adapt and transform the stories from the book series by Snicket and Pullman. However, the Storytel Originals represent a different case of transmedial seriality because these texts not only lend inspiration from popular television series and other serial media, but they also develop the serial form and content of these texts in order to make them fit the format and intended audience of the digital audiobook. The audiobook has become increasingly widespread in recent years, a development that may first and foremost be explained by the process of digitalization, which has changed the way audiobooks are produced, distributed, and

DOI: 10.4324/9781003265894-5

consumed.[1] Accordingly, audiobooks are currently one of the only areas within the publishing field that experiences actual growth. Most recently, the format's success has culminated with the emergence of born-audio, or audio first, narratives, as exemplified by Storytel's Originals series. These productions thus represent how the publishing industry currently responds to digitalization by producing content that fits emerging formats and new digital distribution models.

I argue that serialization, in this context, becomes a central commercial and narrative strategy. Accordingly, I examine how Storytel, as a leading actor on the international book market, uses the serial format to make the digital audiobook "instantly popular," recalling Hagedorn's argument discussed in my introduction.[2] That is, they use the format to cultivate and maintain an audience for the streaming platform. Focusing on Storytel's use of the serial format, this chapter will contribute to this book's overall project by investigating the connection between serialization as a narrative strategy in the Originals series and the medial and commercial aspects of serial publishing. I first examine how the serial format functions in relation to the developing format of the audiobook. I analyze Storytel Originals as a brand, focusing on the general characteristics of the born-audio series. Specifically, I examine how these texts move between different media logics and traditions: They are, at once, returning to the classic format of feuilleton novels and imitating the logics of other serial media. Accordingly, the case of the Originals series may be related to discussions in the previous chapters about the tension, in many serial narratives, between adjusting to the logics of media convergence and emphasizing the continuing relevance of medium specificity. The case of Storytel and the Originals series illustrate how the boundary between literature and other media is blurring at the level of narrative content and when it comes to modes of production and distribution. However, while Jim Collins insists that serial narratives are no longer medium-specific,[3] I argue that the medium still matters. In this case, I demonstrate how the medial and commercial context of the digital audiobook is central to how Storytel develops its serial narrative content.

To demonstrate how different media logics play out in relation to specific serial born-audio texts, I analyze the Original series *Virus* by the Swedish author Daniel Åberg. *Virus* was published in seven seasons from 2016 to 2020 and is among the most popular Storytel Originals in Sweden and worldwide. The series has been translated into several languages, including English, Dutch, Finnish, and even the Indian dialect Marathi.[4] Examining the narrative content, the medial framing, and the reception of the series in terms of listener response, I investigate how Åberg and Storytel use the serial format to build an audience for the story and the platform.

The Audiobook Boom and Storytel Originals

Storytel's born-audio productions and their use of the serial format must be considered in relation to a broader development: the increasing popularity of audiobooks.[5] Audiobooks are nothing new: the format may be traced back to the invention of the phonograph in the 19th century. In the 20th century, audiobooks were primarily seen as an aid for the visually impaired and those with reading disabilities: As explored by Matthew Rubery, the history and use of the format are linked to the history of disability.[6] However, since the turn of the millennium, the format has entered the broader and more commercially oriented field of publishing. While audiobooks traditionally had the status of a secondary medium, remediating the content of the printed book and targeted primarily toward those who could not read in other ways, the format has now become widespread. This so-called "audiobook boom" was triggered by digitalization, which has made audiobooks easier and cheaper to produce and distribute and furthermore implies new possibilities of accessing and consuming literature.[7] Digital distribution services such as Storytel and Audible make it possible to access large collections of audiobooks via download or streaming, and portable devices such as smartphones make it possible to listen on the move. As discussed by Iben Have and Birgitte Stougaard Pedersen, the digital audiobook thus paves the way for the integration of literary consumption into everyday life, attracting new readers and resulting in new literary experiences.[8]

This development has, most recently, led to the development of new forms of content. Traditionally, the audiobook is defined as "a remediation of the printed book,"[9] thus, merely as a reformatting of content that already exists in print. Because of the audiobook's status as an aid for those who cannot read, the ambition has often been to get as close as possible to the experience of reading the text, and the performance consequently had to be as neutral as possible.[10] However, following the changing status of the audiobook, we see an increasing interest in developing content that makes use of the affordances of the audiobook format, for example, by including voice dramatization, music, or other sound effects.[11] Amazon's audiobook publisher Audible launched their Audible Originals in 2016, at the same time as Storytel launched their Originals series.[12] Other traditional publishers have followed suit: For instance, in 2020, the Danish publisher Gyldendal launched their new brand of audio first productions, Gyldendal Stereo, suggesting that even very traditional and established publishers have understood the need to invest in the emerging format.

Although a first mover within the field, Storytel is thus far from alone in investing in born-audio content. However, their Originals differ from similar brands because of their explicit use of serial format as a central element in their strategy of adjusting textual content to the audio format. The Originals series are produced by Storytel's publishing company Storyside, and Storytel owns all rights to the texts. While Storytel primarily distributes content produced by other publishers, the Originals reflect their interest in producing original content to attract listeners and compete with similar streaming services and distributors.[13] The series are organized into episodes and seasons: each episode is 50–60 minutes, and each season usually includes ten episodes. Arguably, the serial format functions as a part of Storytel's ambition to produce content that fits the audiobook format and the target groups for this format. On the company's Danish webpage, an Originals series is defined as

> A story that is written directly for sound. This means that you can easily keep track of what's happening in the story, even during the hectic events of everyday life. The reason behind this is that we have noticed that not all written stories reach their full potential as audiobooks. For example, the writing style might be heavy with metaphors, have too many vague characters or a disrupted timeline that stands in the way of the listening experience.[14]

Thus, according to the company, writing directly for sound means that the story should be easy to follow "even during the hectic events of everyday life." This idea reflects the widespread assumption that audiobook consumers are more easily distracted than readers of printed books because consumption of audiobooks may, and often does, occur while doing something else.[15] Whether it is actually true that audiobook listeners prefer this type of text may be debated; many listeners report that they often listen to audiobooks while not moving, for instance, in bed, and that they are concentrated when listening.[16] However, the assumption that audiobooks should be easy to follow is widespread in the public debate and within the publishing industry. Publishers often approach the format with an eye to the new target groups that may be reached because of the potential for multitasking and associate the format with plot-centered stories that are easy to follow in popular genres such as romance and crime fiction.

Storytel's use of the serial format in the Originals series may be considered in this context. A report from Storytel in 2018 states that organizing narrative content in short episodes fits well with consumption on the move.[17] The report notes that the short episodes fit the presumed "diminishing attention spans" of the users.[18] While this idea may, again, be debated, the statement reflects the company's ambition to produce content that resonates with new user groups and with the logics of digital culture. At the same time, the Originals may also be connected with the historical feuilleton format.

As noted in my introduction, seriality has been historically associated with popular genres such as those represented by the Originals. Explaining the Originals format, Storytel writes,

> Every episode has its own dramaturgical storytelling universe, while at the same time following the main story of the season. This means that you, the listener, can look forward to a story filled with more intense moments and cliffhangers. The format isn't new in the literary world and was actually used as early as the 19th century with classics such as Sherlock Holmes, Oliver Twist, and several others that got their start as serials in the English newspapers.[19]

Invoking the 19th-century serial classics, the service associates their new brand with an aspect of continuity. The organization of the texts in "episodes" and "seasons" may resonate with the world of television series, yet Storytel also connects the Originals to literary tradition. It is certainly possible to point out similarities between the born-audio and 19th-century feuilleton novels. As noted by Matthew Rubery, many 19th-century novels were written to be read aloud, as Victorian literary culture was, to a great extent, a culture of performative and social reading. Rubery traces continuities between contemporary audiobook consumption and the Victorian reading culture and concludes that "one of the most consequential effects of the new digital audio has been to bring back old ways of reading, specifically the practice of reading aloud associated with the nineteenth century parlour."[20] His primary example is the works of Charles Dickens, who often performed his texts at public reading events.[21] Dickens' works are also a central example of historical serial fiction, and the case accordingly demonstrates how serialization has historically been associated with read-aloud texts. Illustrating this connection, the Originals series share certain textual features with historical feuilletons: They often include much dialogue, which is well suited for oral performance, and tend to use cliffhangers and other narrative features to maintain the readers' attention across episodes or chapters.[22]

Beyond the textual level, it is possible to point to similarities in how larger media platforms use the old and new serials, that is, in the uses of seriality as a business strategy. According to Hagedorn, feuilletons in the 19th century were used to attract readers to a new mass medium—printed journals and newspapers. From the opposite perspective, authors often used the serial format to reach those readers who could not afford to buy printed books. After the initial publication in feuilleton format, all installments were collected and published as bound novels. Storytel uses the Originals series in a similar way: their subscription-based model and the audio format make it possible to reach a broad audience, including readers who do not usually read books, while the most popular Originals series are also published as printed books.[23] Moreover, like the old newspapers, Storytel arguably uses the serial format to secure the readers' loyalty to the service. Like newspapers, subscription-based streaming services are dependent on readers to return for more. The serial format is ideal for making listeners return to, and keep them on, the platform over a longer time. That is, as Karl Berglund and Ann Steiner point out, the serial format serves to maintain listeners' interest, not only in new titles on the streaming platform but also in the vast backlist catalog offered on the platform. "When a book is published, the older ones in the series receive attention and many choose to start with one of the earlier books," Berglund and Steiner note. "New titles are the driving force, but it is their ability to pull streaming from older titles that creates high numbers of streams as a whole and makes the backlist concept advantageous."[24]

Accordingly, Storytel's use of the serial format reflects the logic described by Hagedorn and quoted in the introduction of this book. Hagedorn observes how producers have "consistently turned to the serial form of narrative presentation precisely in order to cultivate a dependable audience of consumers" and concludes that new serials "function not only to increase newspaper circulation, the sale of theatre tickets, or increasingly expensive advertising spots, but more significantly they serve to *promote the medium in which they appear*."[25] As 19th-century newspapers used serials to cultivate a readership, not only for that specific series or newspaper but also for the medium of print—and as radio and television used the format in the 20th century—so does Storytel, arguably, use the Originals series to cultivate a readership for the platform and digital audiobooks. While the audiobook might not in itself be defined as a new mass medium, its recent popularity and the new forms of usage brought about by digitalization justify that we apply Hagedorn's argument to the audio-born serials.

The fact that Storytel uses the serial format in this way is supported by the aforementioned report, emphasizing the significance of seriality as a competitive strategy in modern media culture. The report states,

> In a highly competitive environment—fighting to occupy users' free time—producers and distributors of content depend more than ever on the engagement of the services they offer. The sustained, consistent, and recurring consumption of narrative series has demonstrated its effectiveness above any other format (such as short videos or movies) in building up that engagement.[26]

Thus, reflecting the logic pointed out by Hagedorn, the serial format is supposed to secure "sustained, consistent, and recurring consumption" in competition not only with other audiobook distributors or book retailers but also with any producer and distributor of content. This competition is framed by a situation in which producers are fighting "to occupy users' free time." While in the 19th century, authors mainly used the serial format to get to those readers who could not afford printed books, the capital that matters most in this contemporary context is time. Audiobooks have an advantage in this competition because of the format's medial affordances and potential for multitasking. The Originals are targeted toward readers who do not have time to read books, hence framing the series as stories that fit into "the hectic events of everyday life."

The quote from the report reflects Storytel's orientation toward the broad entertainment industry. While literary production and publishing have historically functioned separately from other forms of media production, the case of the Originals series illustrates the blurring of these boundaries in a modern convergence culture. Despite the marked connection to 19th-century literature, the use of the serial format in these productions stresses this orientation. That is, the Originals are targeted toward an audience that may not primarily identify as readers. Focusing on the Originals series' inspiration from television series, Iben Have and Mille Raabye Jensen write,

> The format will . . . lure readers to a literary format. At the same time, they lend concepts and working methods from the television series in order to produce a new understanding of the content and use of audio series. The strategy is . . . to accommodate the new forms of consumption in an on-demand culture and reflect the overall media tendencies . . . in order to thus make literature and audiobooks even more attractive, packing it as a television series.[27]

As suggested by Have and Raabye Jensen, Storytel's inspiration from television series is evident not only in the labeling of installments as "episodes" and "seasons" but also in their production methods: Series are often produced collectively, and the author becomes a "writer," losing his or her central role and status in relation to the literary text. This change in power relation is most notably reflected in the fact that Storytel owns the copyrights for the series. Accordingly, the Originals series becomes associated with changing power relations between authors, publishers, and distributors in contemporary publishing culture.[28] These changes become evident at a paratextual level in relation to the Originals: Promotion of these series often focuses on the performer, usually an actor, who reads the story, rather than on the series author, and some covers do not even include the author's name. Storytel, in many cases, produces book trailers to the series, which also contribute to visualize and dramatize the stories.[29] Furthermore, as a part of their adjustment to the audio format, many series include sound effects: Musical intros and outros at the beginning and end of each episode, for instance, again refer to the packing of television series.

While Storytel's Originals thus seems oriented toward the logics of television series, Storytel has also adjusted their use of the serial format to the medial affordances of audiobook, realizing that people do not listen to audiobooks in the same way as they watch television series. As explored by Elisa Wallin and Jan Nolin, people usually listen to audiobooks during the day, in everyday situations: not during "prime time," in the evening.[30] Supporting this argument, Have and Raabye Jensen describe the phenomenon of "audio bingeing": Rather than listening to one episode at a time, people tend to listen for hours.[31] Realizing this, Storytel has begun to produce their Originals series in a different format than the 10-episode format they initially launched: Now, all episodes in a season are often released in one audio file, rather than in ten separate files. The music at the beginning and end of each episode has disappeared. The result is something that looks like a traditional novel in audiobook format. Storytel editor, Anna Öqvist Ragnar comments,

> The episodic format has proved harder to implement than we thought it would be. [M]y hypothesis from the beginning was that the episodic format functions very well in television series. . . . People are used to it. You don't have to dedicate yourself to listening for ten hours straight but can just have a try for an hour. And it is very possible that people do that, but the problem is that then, they jump off, they kind of get nine chances to jump off the series. . . . The competition is too fierce for us to allow that anymore. So now, we just want to get them going and not give them any single chance to jump off.[32]

This lesson seems to suggest that serial narratives are, indeed, still medium-specific, shaped by the media cultures that surround them. While borrowing from the serial media of television and podcasts, the audiobook industry needs to adjust to the conventions of reading and book publishing, which still, to a great extent, shape the engagement with their products. Ragnar further speculates that, contrary to the usual television audience, which may be oriented toward the short format of the film, the literary audience will be used to long formats such as novels and not be scared away by the prospect of a 10-hour-long audio file.[33] Accordingly, it appears that the format of audio-born serials leads Storytel not only to imitate other media but also to reinvent the traditional novel.

The Serial Virus

Daniel Åberg's Originals series *Virus* exemplifies the development described previously. As one of the first Originals series to be published in Sweden, *Virus* reflects the format's original orientation toward other media, especially television series, but as one of the longest Originals series, developing across seven seasons, it has also lived through the adjustments of the use of the format described earlier. The series is about a deadly virus, which breaks out in Stockholm and kills almost all of humanity in a few days. It follows a small group of survivors, focusing first and foremost on the process of survival. Thus, it represents a story that has been popular ever since *Robinson Crusoe* and that has recently been exemplified in such successful television series as *Lost* and *The Walking Dead*—an explicit reference to the latter is included in *Virus*. The emphasis on survival results in a plot-driven, action-filled story, with cliffhangers carefully placed at the end of almost every episode and season. Accordingly, the *Virus* series exemplifies the kind of straightforward, plot-driven story that Storytel wants to promote with the Originals brand.

While copying a televisions series logic, the *Virus* series relates to seriality in a broader sense: The series itself appears as a continuation of Åberg's previous works, the novels *Dannyboy och kärleken* (2005) and *Vi har redan sagt hejdå* (2011). Åberg draws attention to the serial aspect in a post on Storytel's blog in 2017.[34] Some of the central characters from these previous novels live on the post-apocalyptic story. This connection is interesting most of all because it displays how the serial story is transformed across volumes and especially as it is adjusted to a new medial context. The previous works are characterized by style experiments that are strongly linked to the logics of the printed book: *Vi har redan sagt hejdå*, for instance, plays with temporality and scatters the order of the chapters so that the reader has to piece the chronology of the story together.[35] This structure starkly contrasts with the "straightforward" storyline in the *Virus* series. The contrast between the two works draws attention to how the new format influences Åberg's writing. Åberg himself describes how he adjusts his writing to the Originals format:

> When I write my audiobook serials. . . . I always try to be clear and guide the listener by making sure that it is easy to understand where and when we are in the story and who is there. In a series like *Virus*, for instance, I usually have two or three parallel plotlines going, and my protagonists are situated in different places. . . . In new chapters, I try as quickly as possible to re-establish the place and remind listeners about who is where and why.[36]

Åberg points to a repetitive element in his series and frames it as a way to accommodate the intended listening situation—where people cannot go back and reread the text as easily as with printed books. Notably, similar strategies can be observed in most serial fiction where authors want to remind readers of what happened in previous installments—for the same reason as recaps are used in television series. Thus, the attempt to produce a text that is well suited for the audio format, in this case, results in a text that makes use of established narrative techniques within serial fiction.

Åberg thus adjusts the text to the serial audiobook format, and the *Virus* series, accordingly, reflects the connection between a narrative and a medial aspect of serialization: How seriality shapes textual content across media and format. However, to examine how the narrative strategies are connected to the commercial use of the format, it is necessary to look at the reception of the series. The remaining part of this analysis accordingly focuses on serial listener behavior. Listeners' responses to the series may be studied through listeners' feedback and comments to the series posted in the Storytel app. In the app, when you finish a book, a window pops up asking you to review the book according to a system focusing on emotional response: "How would you describe the book based on feelings," the app asks, and the reader is asked to evaluate the book using a range of different emojis and rating it with a number of stars. Finally, it is possible to post a comment. Most people responded positively to *Virus* with an average of four stars for the entire series. They indicate that the series was a "page-turner" (one of the emoji categories), reflecting Åberg's explicit use of the serial format to present cliffhangers and create suspense. Several users also post comments that reflect positively on the use of the serial format.

Storytel's explicit focus in the app on promoting listener feedback suggests how they actively seek to encourage the kind of participatory culture that historically surrounds serial narratives. Notably, the listener comments and statistics on ratings of the books are visible in the app, enabling other potential listeners to see what others think of the book. Accordingly, the listener feedback is used to promote the book in question: The effect becomes especially strong in relation to serial fiction since most dissatisfied listeners will stop listening—and commenting—as the series continues. Later installments of a series accordingly often receive positive feedback: The later *Virus* seasons have the highest ratings of all (while the lowest number of listeners). Storytel's promotional use of the listeners' ratings exemplifies a commercial use of participatory culture, which will also be discussed in Chapter 6 of this book in relation to the case of Wattpad.

Of course, not all readers of serial narratives participate actively. Usually, only a small percentage of all readers of a given work chooses to engage by commenting or rating. Commenting on the aspect of participation in serial cultures, Frank Kelleter points out how serial audiences may operate as *"agents of narrative continuation"*—even "when readers 'do' nothing but read, because the sphere of production will then automatically make inferences about their behavior as *customers*; a drop in sales thus becomes a reader's response."[37] This concept of indirect influence is also exemplified by the case of Storytel Originals, where audience response to the series in the form of data on listener behavior, whether or not they keep listening, may affect the producer's decision about whether the series should be allowed to continue.[38] The mere fact that the *Virus* series has been allowed to continue in many seasons, seven in total, thus reflects its success.

Elsewhere, I have analyzed data on listener behavior in relation to the *Virus* series, together with Julia Pennlert.[39] Our results shows that the series was relatively successful in terms of attracting and maintaining listeners on Storytel.[40] The study quoted later notably represents the series' popularity at a specific time: in August 2019. Since the series continues to be available on the platform, the numbers have changed since then, especially since 2020, where the release of the *Virus* finale and a pandemic influenced the popularity of series, as I discuss later in this chapter.

According to Storytel's 2019 data, more than 30,000 users began listening to *Virus*'s first season. Usually, first volumes or episodes in serials have the most reads, since people who read later episodes will also have read the previous installments. Most drop-offs—when people stop reading—will also be in relation to the first episode. In the case of *Virus*, out of a total number of 31,343 listeners who began listening to the first episode, only 16.217 listened through to the end. However, after this initial drop, the number of listenings stabilized around 10–15,000 per season, which is high for a Swedish audiobook. There are no big drops in the number of listeners between seasons. It appears that Åberg's suspense-driven narrative successfully maintains listeners to the series, and thus, on the service.[41]

The success of the *Virus* series is reflected in the fact that it was continued in what at first appeared as a spin-off: The series *Smittad*, which spans three new seasons. *Smittad* is presented as a continuation of the story presented in *Virus*. *Virus* seasons 1–4 presented an intense story about four characters' experiences of the virus outbreak in Stockholm. *Smittad* focuses on the same group of survivors yet takes off a few months after *Virus* ended. New characters are introduced, and the setting is expanded as a part of the story now unfolds in the city of Kiruna. The series also got a new performing narrator: While *Virus* 1–4 were read by the Swedish actress, Disa Östram, *Smittad* is performed by the actress Philomène Grandin. This change presents *Smittad* as a different work than *Virus*, considering the fact that the performing narrator is central in the framing of the audiobook.[42] On the covers of the first four *Virus* seasons, Disa Östram is pictured, posing as one of the central characters in the series. Similarly, Grandin is presented on the covers for the *Smittad* series. Thus, the covers support an interpretation of the performer and her voice as a part of the work.

Smittad thus at several levels represents a disruption in the *Virus* series when it comes to narrative content as well as paratextual framing and performance. The listener's reactions to *Smittad* in the Storytel app indicate a general dissatisfaction with these changes. Many users comment on the new narrator, and the shift in the narrator is experienced as confusing. While nobody complains about Grandin's performance, the comments emphasize how the shift in narrator produces a disruption in the sense of serial continuity: Seemingly, serial listeners value this aspect of continuity very highly, and in audiobooks, the performing voice becomes a central aspect of establishing this sense of continuity. That is, the voice contributes to established serial recognition—the sense of returning, not only to a serial storyworld and specific fictional characters but also to the specific voice of the performing narrator. Furthermore, a few people comment on their confusion about the introduction of new characters. This hint of dissatisfaction may explain the decreasing numbers of listenings to the new series: The first episode in the first season of *Smittad*, had, in 2019, 10,754 listenings, but the season hereafter had many dropouts. Only 6,128 listeners listened through the first season. By August 2019, only 1,754 had listened through the two whole seasons of *Smittad*, which had then been published. Thus, at this point, the series seemed to have lost its ability to maintain listeners, arguably because of a lack of narrative continuity between the spin-off and the original series.[43]

The third and final season in the *Virus* spin-off series, *Smittad*, was supposed to be released on Storytel in spring 2020. It was released in May 2020, however, not with the planned title, *Smittad 3*. Instead, the new season was released as *Virus 7*, and the two previous seasons in the *Smittad* series, *Smittad* 1 and 2 were nowhere to be found in the Storytel app: They had been renamed *Virus* 5 and 6, respectively. This change of title reframes the series previously known as *Smittad* as a direct continuation of the first four *Virus* seasons: It is now one series instead of two. In this way, Storytel uses the serial paratexts, especially the change of title, to emphasize the aspect of narrative continuity that was felt by some users to be missing in the new series. Furthermore, the last season, *Virus 7*, marks a return to the original protagonists in the first *Virus* series, further stressing this aspect of continuity. Notably, the shift in the title also works to promote the original four seasons since the new season generates new attention toward them, following the logic described by Berglund and Steiner. Many comments in the app to the first seasons suggest that many new listeners listened in 2020, a fact confirmed by Åberg.[44] This fact suggests how serial publishing, combined with Storytel's digital distribution model, paves the way for what Chris Anderson calls the "long-tail" logic on the contemporary book market: Where it is possible to store and potentially access and sell products years after they were published.[45]

The 2020 increase in the number of listeners to the *Virus* series may also be related to the fact that the conclusion of the series coincided with the outbreak of the Covid-19 epidemic in spring 2020—making the series about a global pandemic more relevant than ever. When asked about this situation, Åberg is reluctant to answer. He does not want to benefit from the pandemic yet admits that it led to increasing attention toward the series; for instance, Storytel promoted the series in their "selected books of the week" category in the app in March 2020.[46] Arguably, the change of title for the *Smittad* series may also be considered in this context, as the word *Virus* connoted relevance in 2020. Furthermore, Storytel, like other streaming services, experienced a general increase in users in 2020. Consumption of books in digital formats, including audiobooks, increased significantly in both Sweden and Denmark during the pandemic, arguably because many preferred digitally distributed books in a situation with restricted access to physical bookstores or libraries.[47] The case of Åberg's *Virus* accordingly demonstrates how the serial publishing format, combined with the digital distribution model via streaming, means that external factors, such as a global pandemic, may continuously influence the popularity and sales of series.

Conclusion: Born-Audio Seriality

The case of Storytel Originals illustrates the general tendency examined in this book: A resurgence and development of the serial narrative format as literary works move across media. While the Originals concept at first glance signals a return to the feuilleton format that dominated 19th-century literary culture, Storytel also develops the serial format as they import the logics of other serial media such as television series and podcasts. In this way, they illustrate how literature is influenced by other media logics in contemporary media culture. Furthermore, Storytel adjusts the series to the specific affordances of the digital audiobook. Of course, it may be debated whether the resulting serial texts, such as Åberg's *Virus*, reflect how the audiobook as a medial format shapes literary content—or whether it is instead Storytel's commercial agenda, and their use of the serial form to attract and maintain listeners to the platform that shape these texts. Certainly, it is possible to find examples of audio narratives that are not "straightforward storytelling." Many podcasts, for instance, exemplify more complex narratives.[48] Rather than considering the Originals series merely as an example of how the audiobook shapes literary content, one must consider the series as the result of the combined influence of medium-specific conditions, the author's esthetic choices and narrative strategies—and, not least, the producer and distributor, Storytel's, agenda, which furthermore reflects the conditions of the digitalized book market. Accordingly, the case illustrates the use of serialization in digital culture to secure "consistent, sustained, and recurrent consumption"[49] of content on digital platforms and streaming services.

In the later chapter on seriality on Wattpad, I further discuss this commercial aspect in relation to the social and participatory dimension of serial culture. Audiobooks are not considered social media: Listeners usually listen on their own. However, Storytel does encourage participation in the form of user feedback in the app. The service also administrates audiobook groups on Facebook, where people discuss audiobooks and authors promote their books. This kind of social interaction generates attention and, thus, commercial value for the company.

The success of Storytel's serial publishing model is demonstrated by Åberg's *Virus* series, which has been able to maintain a large number of listeners across seven seasons. Of course, it is also possible to point to less successful series, and the whole process, in the case of the *Virus* series, of turning two series into one reflects the continuous work-in-progress format of the digitally distributed series. The born-audio format is still emerging as I am writing this in 2021, and Storytel and similar actors in the publishing industry are continuously developing the serial format as they realize how it may be adjusted to the medium and target groups.

This ongoing process of revising content reflects how the serial format is developed across media. In Chapter 2, I discussed Jim Collins's argument that serialized narratives are no longer medium-specific.[50] However, the case of the Originals supports my argument that, indeed, they are. While Storytel may want to attract users of television series, people do not listen to audiobooks the same way as they watch television series. Therefore, the producer needs to balance between producing recognizability, using such concepts as seasons and episodes, and adjusting to the specific affordances of the audiobook medium—for instance, reflected in their abandoning of the 50-minute episodic format. Future studies may continue to examine the emerging category of texts that result from this ongoing development. While Storytel seems to be returning to a traditional audiobook format, with all episodes in one audio file, it is also possible to observe new kinds of born-audio experiments, which include sound effects, music, and voice dramatization. Whether or not this new category of texts may also, in the future, be linked to the serial format is hard to say. As the case of Dickens's feuilleton novels tells us, serialization often does go hand in hand with stories written to be performed out loud, and the current rise of serialized audio narratives, podcasts, as well as audiobooks, also suggests that the format works well for telling stories through sound. The rest depends on the development of the market, the media, and the listeners.

Notes

1. Iben Have and Birgitte Stougaard Pedersen, *Digital Audiobooks: New Users, Media and Experiences* (New York: Routledge, 2016).
2. Roger Hagedorn, "Technology and Economic Exploitation: The Serial as a Form of Narrative Presentation," *Wide Angle* 10, no. 4 (1988): 5.
3. Jim Collins, "The Use Values of Narrativity in Digital Cultures," *New Literary History* 44 (2013): 653.
4. In fact, several of these translations are, rather, adaptations, as the setting and the characters, names, etc., are changed to reflect the new local context—for instance, the Dutch version, *Virus: Amsterdam* takes place in Amsterdam. For more on Storytel's practice of adjusting stories to local contexts, see Sara Tanderup Linkis, "Läsning i rörelse. Platsens betydelse i Storytels ljudfodda berättelser," in *Från Stringberg till Storytel,* eds. Julia Pennlert and Lars Ilshammar (Stockholm: Daidalos, 2021), 269–94.
5. For a discussion of the so-called audiobook boom, see, e.g., Boris Kashka, "Audiobooks Are the New Ebooks. Except They Might Keep Growing," *Vulture,* September 20, 2018, www.vulture.com/2018/09/audiobooks-are-booming-but-how-long-will-that-last.html; Matthew Rubery, "Play It Again, Sam Weller. New Digital Audiobooks and Old Ways of Reading," *Journal of Victorian Culture* 13, no. 1 (2010): 58–79.
6. Matthew Rubery, *The Untold History of the Talking Book* (Cambridge, MA: Harvard University Press, 2016).
7. Have and Stougaard Pedersen, *Digital Audiobooks.*
8. Ibid.
9. Ibid., 7.
10. For further discussion of this tradition, see Cecilia Björkén Nyberg, "Tolkning, tydlighed och tolkande tydlighet. Tre röstgestaltningar av Hjalmar Söderbergs *Den allvarsamma leken,*" in *Från Stringberg till Storytel,* eds. Julia Pennlert and Lars Ilshammar (Stockholm: Daidalos, 2021), 137–61.
11. This development may also be related to the rising popularity of podcasts, another form of audio narratives which are often serialized. Indeed, the new emphasis on born-audio productions may also reflect the audiobook industry's orientation toward a growing podcast audience, although born-audio serials are characterized by a "scripted" quality, as opposed to the spoken, improvised style associated with podcasts.
12. For an analysis of the Audible Originals concept, see Birgitte Stougaard Pedersen, "At skrive gennem lyd," *Passage* 83 (2020): 85–99.
13. For a discussion of the production of original content by streaming services for books, see Karl Berglund and Sara Tanderup Linkis, "Modelling Subscription-Based Services for Books," *Memoires du Livre/Studies in Book Culture* (forthcoming).
14. "Hvad er Mofibo Originals," *Mofibo Support,* June 22, 2021, https://support.mofibo.com/hc/da/articles/115001070410-Hvad-er-en-Mofibo-Original. Translated from Danish by the author.
15. Have and Stougaard Pedersen, *Digital Audiobooks.*
16. Ibid. See also the 2019 report form the Swedish Publisher's Association for statistics on the habits and uses of audiobooks by Swedish consumers. The report concludes that many audiobook users listen to audiobooks, not because of its multitasking potential, but because it gives them a sense of human presence.

Hedda Hanner, Alice O'Connor and Erik Wikberg, *Ljudboken. Hur den Digitala Logiken påverkar Marknaden, Konsumptionen och Framtiden* (Stockholm: Svenska Förläggareföreningen, 2019), 29.
17. Porter Anderson, "Storytel in Spain: When Entering the Audiobook Market Means Making New Serials," *Publishing Perspectives,* June 6, 2018, https://publishingperspectives.com/2018/06/storytel-spain-audiobook-market-original-serials/.
18. Ibid.
19. Mofibo support.
20. Rubery, "Play it again," 74.
21. Ibid.
22. For further examples of how the Storytel Originals are written to fit audio consumption, see Daniel Åberg, "At skrive til øret. Betragtninger fra en Storytel Originals forfatter," *Passage* 83 (2020): 71–84.
23. As several authors point out, writing Originals series for Storytel becomes a possibility to reach a new audience and gain economic capital. This aspect, which was also central to many 19th-century writers of popular fiction, is stressed by the author Daniel Åberg, who describes how Storytel offered him a considerable fee for writing an Originals series, "more than what is usual within the publishing business." Åberg, "Betragtninger," 68.
24. Karl Berglund and Ann Steiner, "Is Backlist the New Frontlist," *Logos* 32, no. 1 (2021): 14.
25. Hagedorn, "Technology," 5.
26. Anderson, "New Serials."
27. Iben Have and Mille Raabye Jensen, "Audiobingeing. Storytel Originals som produkt af en streaming kultur," *Passage* 83 (2020): 82. Translated from Danish by the author.
28. For further reflections on the way in which digital audiobook influences the logics of the publishing field, see Iben Have and Birgitte Stougaard Pedersen, "The Audiobook Circuit in Digital Publishing: Voicing the Silent Revolution," *New Media & Society* 22, no. 3 (2020): 409–28. For reflecting, specifically, on the influence of subscription-based streaming on the relations between literary actors, see Berglund and Tanderup Linkis, "Modelling."
29. For a further analysis of Storytel's book trailers, see Sara Tanderup Linkis, "Resonant Listening. Local Voices and Places in Born-Audio Literary Narratives," in *Resonance and the Echo Chamber of Reading,* ed. Shuangyi Li, *Canadian Review of Comparative Literature/Revue canadienne de littérature compare* 47, no. 4 (2021): 404–23; Tanderup Linkis, "Läsning i rörelse," 282.
30. Jan Nolin and Elisa Wallin, "Time to Read: Exploring the Time Spaces of Subscription-Based Audiobooks," *New Media & Society* 22, no. 3 (2020): 1–19.
31. Have and Raabye Jensen, "Audio-Bingeing."
32. Anna Öqvist Ragnar, in interview by Karl Berglund. Cited in Berglund and Tanderup Linkis, "Modelling."
33. Ragnar, in interview by Karl Berglund. Cited in Berglund and Tanderup Linkis, "Modelling."
34. Daniel Åberg, "Virus författaren avslöjer detaljer vi kan ha missat!" *Storytel's blog,* 2017, https://blog.storytel.se/2017/04/13/virus-forfattaren-avslojar-detaljer-vi-kan-ha-missat/.
35. *Vi har redan sagt hejdå* has also been produced in audiobook format, performed by the author; however, in audio format, it is difficult to piece the story together—since you do not have the physical book to look back and reread.

36. Åberg, "Betragtninger," 71.
37. Frank Kelleter, "Five Ways of Looking at Popular Seriality," in *Media of Serial Narratives,* ed. Frank Kelleter (Columbus: The Ohio State University Press, 2017), 13.
38. In their presentation of the brand for potential authors, Storytel emphasizes how the production process, they are "supported by data but without limiting creative freedom." "Originals," *Storytel Publishing* (2021), https://publishing.storytel.com/sg/originals/.
39. Sara Tanderup Linkis and Julia Pennlert, "Episodic Listening. A Study of the Usage of Serialized Audiobooks," *Journal of Electronic Publishing* 3, no. 20, https://doi.org/10.3998/3336451.0023.102. The article is based on pseudonymized data, provided by Storytel, making it possible to study the number of listeners to the work in question, how long people listen, statistically, and when they stop listening.
40. Notably, the numbers presented later formally refer to the numbers of *listenings*. Since the data are anonymized, it is not possible to see whether some listeners listen to the series several times. However, the number of listenings will, reasonably, also reflect the actual number of listeners to the series.
41. Tanderup Linkis and Pennlert, "Episodic."
42. For reflections on the voice of the performing narrator, see Have and Stougaard Pedersen, *Digital Audiobooks,* 79–94. See also a recent study of Swedish audiobook consumers, by Pennlert and Tanderup Linkis, where the majority of Swedish audiobook consumers point to the performer as an important factor when choosing books to listen to. Sara Tanderup Linkis and Julia Pennlert, "It Adds a Dimension" (paper presented at the conference "Revolutions in Reading," Stockholm University, Stockholm, June 22, 2021).
43. Tanderup Linkis and Pennlert, "Episodic."
44. Daniel Åberg, "Daniel Åberg skrev ljudbokserie om dödligt virus men skulle aldrig kalla sig virusexpert," interview by Sölvé Dahlgren, *Bokugg,* March 16, 2020, www.boktugg.se/2020/03/16/daniel-aberg-skrev-ljudboksserie-om-dodligt-virus-men-skulle-aldrig-kalla-sig-virusexpert/.
45. Chris Anderson, "The Long Tail," *Wired Magazine,* January 10, 2004, www.wired.com/2004/10/tail/. For further reflections on this logic specifically in relation to serial publishing, see Berglund and Steiner, "New Frontlist."
46. Åberg, "Virusexpert."
47. See Erik Wikberg, *Bokförsäljningsstatistiken: Helåret 2020* (Stockholm: Svenska Förläggareföreningen, 2021). *Bogen og litteraturens vilkår: Bogpanelets årsrapport 2020* (Slots- og kulturstyrelsen, 2020), https://boghandlerforeningen.dk/wp-content/uploads/2020/11/bogen-og-litteraturens-vilkaar-2020.pdf.
48. Certain podcasts may even appear more "literary" than the Originals series, when it comes to the framing and serial paratexts: installments in the popular podcast "Serial" is for instance labeled as "chapters," as opposed to the "episodes" in the Storytel Originals series.
49. Anderson, "New Serials."
50. Collins, "Use Values," 653.

6 "Ilysm!" Serial Writing and Social Reading on Wattpad

In 2013, the Canadian author Margaret Atwood published a serial novel, *The Happy Zombie Sunrise Home*, together with the younger author, Naomi Alderman. The publication was remarkable, not only because the story was about zombies (!) and because it was the result of an unusual collaboration between two authors from different generations, but also because it was published on the Canadian website Wattpad, a social platform for aspiring young authors to write and publish their stories. Atwood motivated her decision to publish with Wattpad by referring to the fact that the site promoted a democratic aspect of literary culture. "No one needs to know how old you are, what your social background is, or where you live," she noted and emphasized how "everything on the site is free."[1] The social dimension of the site was supported by its use of a serial publication format, encouraging writers and readers to publish, access, and comment on the stories continuously, chapter by chapter. "Like Dickens during his serial publication of *Pickwick*, Wattpad writers get feedback from readers, and may shape their stories accordingly,"[2] wrote Atwood, comparing the Wattpad community to the active reading cultures surrounding 19th-century serial novels. As professional writers publishing their novel in a serial format via Wattpad, Atwood and Alderman thus appear to blur the boundaries between digital culture and literary tradition, as well as between amateur and professional writing.

In this chapter, I explore the social aspect of serial publishing and reading in digital culture. As mentioned in my introduction and further discussed in Chapter 2, serial narratives are often surrounded by participatory cultures: Ever since Dickens's readers gathered around weekly installments of *The Old Curiosity Shop*, readers have socialized around ongoing serial narratives. The chapter explores how the social aspect of serial reading and writing is developed in the digital age by focusing on the case of Wattpad and by analyzing the social interaction presented in and surrounding two serial Wattpad-novels, Margaret Atwood and Naomi Alderman's *The*

DOI: 10.4324/9781003265894-6

Happy Zombie Sunrise Home (2013) and Anna Todd's *After* (2014). While both of these works were written specifically for publication on Wattpad, they exemplify different uses of the serial format by two already established authors and by an (eventually successful) amateur writer, respectively. By comparing the two cases, I can examine how serialization works in different ways on the platform and how different approaches to the format result in different social dynamics and reader cultures.

As noted by Atwood, user-generated writing sites such as Wattpad at first glance use the serial format to promote the idea of a democratic literary culture, where writers and readers may share and develop their stories continuously and for free. In this way, the site seemingly undermines the commercial aspect of popular seriality that is emphasized by Kelleter and Hagedorn, and which has been explored previously in this book, especially in relation to the case of Storytel, where serialization is used as a strategy to keep readers listening and stories selling. As a free site, Wattpad is based on a culture of sharing. The site reflects the development toward a more active and creative reader in digital literary culture, as discussed by, for example, Claire Squires and Padmini Ray Murray.[3] Murray and Squires note how readers in a digital culture increasingly turn into "prosumers" as they participate in the production of works, for example, by writing fan fiction or book reviews, or indeed, leaving comments and feedback on sites such as Wattpad.[4] This development reflects the broader turn toward participatory culture, which Henry Jenkins associates with modern convergence culture. He summarizes this development as follows:

> If old consumers were assumed to be passive, the new consumer is active. If old consumers were predictable and stationary, then new consumers are migratory, showing a declining loyalty to networks or even media. If old consumers were isolated individuals, then new consumers are more socially connected. If old consumers were seen as compliant, then new consumers are resistant, taking media into their own hands. If the work of media consumers was once silent and invisible, they are now noisy and public.[5]

Jenkins connects this turn toward an active consumer to the development of modern convergence culture, characterized by transmedial production, distribution, and consumption of narratives. Embracing the idea of an emerging democratic digital culture, he presents a rather one-sided development from a passive consumer toward a more actively engaged one. Along with him, other scholars emphasize the changing power balance between producers and consumers, or between authors, publishers, and readers, focusing on the emergence of a grassroots culture, which may potentially disrupt the hierarchies of the traditional publishing system. For instance, Miriam Johnson and Aarthi Vadde both argue that digitalization and social media pave the way for a "citizen author"[6] or amateur writer,[7] whose increasing power disrupts the established publishing system and undermines the traditional publishers' control over the processes of literary canonization.

However, focusing on serialization on Wattpad allows me to complicate this development and provide a more nuanced picture of the effects of digitalization on social reading and serial publishing. Indeed, the history of serialization demonstrates that "old consumers" were not quite as passive as Jenkins would have them be. Serial narratives have never been a one-way business model but have always developed in an interplay between authors, publishers, and users, as has been examined by, among others, Jennifer Hayward, tracing connections between audiences of Victorian serials and television soap operas.[8] Dickens, as mentioned, already received letters from readers, commenting on his novels while they were being published as feuilletons, and he even adjusted the ending of *Great Expectations* according to these comments. The Facebook-based reading culture surrounding *The Familiar*, as discussed in Chapter 2, and the fact that Danielewski uses crowd-funded material in his books, reflects how this tradition may also be linked to contemporary printed serial novels. Frank Kelleter emphasizes this type of interaction between producers and consumers, and the involvement of readers in the production process, as a central characteristic of serial narratives. As cited in chapter 2, he notes how seriality extends the sphere of storytelling into the sphere of story consumption.[9] According to him, series are *"evolving narratives"*, "they can observe their reception and involve it in the act of (dispersed) storytelling itself. Series observe their own effects—they watch their audiences watch them—and react accordingly."[10] Focusing on serialization thus makes it possible to see how social interaction and active audiences were never a new thing; social media and sites such as Wattpad merely make participation easier and provide the framework for interaction between readers and writers across the globe.

An emphasis on seriality may furthermore draw attention to the fact that the social reading cultures that surround serial texts also have a commercial aspect: as also discussed in Chapter 2, in relation to Danielewski's active promotion of reader engagement and social reading on Facebook. Thus, it becomes possible to question the image of Wattpad and similar sites as ideal democratic spaces for social interaction, sharing, and participation. While the concept of participatory culture is often opposed to commercial interests, my analyses will demonstrate how the commercial and social aspects of serialization are connected to the extent that, as noted by Aarthi Vadde, "production and reception—or industrial and quotidian actors—are best understood as *coevolving* forces."[11] That is, complicating Jenkins' argument, it should be emphasized how participatory culture also serves commercial purposes—writing fan fiction or book-blogging turn readers into co-promoters, as noted by Murray and Squires, in tune with the publisher's intention to create "buzz." Despite the proclaimed democratic and participatory potential of social media and digitally distributed serials on Wattpad, the cultural producers or platforms thus remain in control.

In this way, by focusing on the use of digitally distributed serial narratives and the cultures surrounding these narratives on Wattpad, it becomes possible to complicate the perspective on contemporary participatory culture and to investigate how Wattpad's publishing model leads to blurring boundaries not only between amateur users and professional producers but also between social and commercial practices—between cultures of selling and cultures of sharing serial stories.

"The YouTube of Stories": Seriality on Wattpad and Happy Zombies

Wattpad emphasizes its participatory dimension as it presents itself as "The YouTube of Stories."[12] Like YouTube, Wattpad is a user-generated forum, relying on a logic of sharing as unpaid writers provide most of its content. The site was founded by the Canadians Allen Lau and Ivan Yuen in 2006, and by 2021, has more than 90 million users.[13] Membership is free, and Wattpad thus reflects what Aarthi Vadde calls the "mass amateurization of digital publishing";[14] a situation where digitalization has paved the way for amateur writers to publish their writing online or in print without the involvement of professional publishers.

However, while Wattpad is primarily targeted toward amateurs, it is also used by professional writers, including such established names as Margaret Atwood, Dan Brown, and Paulo Coelho, to promote their published works. Other writers have used the site as a gateway to traditional publishing—a well-known example is Anna Todd's bestselling book series *After*, which was discovered as a result of its immense popularity on the site and published by Simon & Schuster. Thus, as noted earlier, Wattpad and similar self-publishing sites blur the boundaries between amateur and professional writing. Here, digital distribution helps readers turn into writers, providing the frames for social interaction about or around literary texts. The use of serial publishing on Wattpad must be considered in this context as it promotes the social uses of the site. Most fiction on Wattpad is published serially, as encouraged by the site's organization. Writers have to upload their texts one chapter at a time, and the texts are also accessed chapter by chapter, with the gaps between chapters being filled out by recommendations of other Wattpad texts or by commercial advertisements. Accordingly, most Wattpad writers publish their chapters continuously as they write them, allowing readers to provide feedback on the ongoing story, possibly affecting its development. Wattpad's guidelines for authors emphasize this type of serial interaction between readers and writers as one of the benefits of using the site. Thus, addressing why writers should use Wattpad, the guidelines say, "When you release your work on Wattpad one chapter at a time, you're rewarded with continual encouragement and real-time feedback from a growing audience, excited to join you for the ride."[15]

The users emphasize this aspect, as they discuss in Wattpad's writer's forums how to get readers or "reads" for their stories. Debating whether to publish a completed work at once or serialize it, one user states, "If you publish it all at once people will read it in one go and be done with it. Post it a chapter at a time, twice a week will be fine. This way you'll build an audience that will follow your work."[16] Another user advises, "Never, ever, post it all at once. This site relies on an algorithm, and to appease it, you have to update at least once a week and at most twice. . . . If you post it all at once, you'll only create a small flicker in the algorithm, and many people will miss you."[17] As it appears from these and many other comments, serialization is used as a strategy to attract and maintain readership. The users' statements are supported by statistical data provided by Melanie Ramdarshan Bold. Having investigated the connection between the number of installments in each story on Wattpad and their popularity, Bold concludes that more installments statistically lead to a larger number of readers and votes.[18] This may be explained by the fact that more installments lead readers to interact more with the text and, most importantly, with each other.

In their guidelines, Wattpad emphasizes the idea of using the serial format to build a loyal readership. While the guidelines for unpublished writers focus on the social aspect, on the possibility of developing one's writing through feedback, the guidelines targeted toward professional authors emphasize the marketing potential of the serial publishing strategy. "Post your first book in a series," it says. "A great way to introduce new readers to your series and drive sales for subsequent books. Many authors serialize the first book in a series, and time it with a new release to create buzz."[19] Thus, digital serialization is presented as a strategy to promote sales of already published works and forthcoming publications.[20] The professional authors' Wattpad pages testify to the fact that this model is widespread. Atwood's novel, *The Heart Goes Last*, is, for instance, available in a chapter-by-chapter format on the site, as are works by such established authors as Dan Brown and Paulo Coelho.

This use of the serial format to build engagement and encourage collaboration between readers and authors is emphasized by several scholars, including Aarthi Vadde, who argues that Wattpad reflects an overall turn toward amateur creativity in digital cultures. She notes,

> Wattpad depends on amateur creativity and interactivity for all of its content and so it encourages serial writing that is spontaneous, frequent, and free-flowing. Wattpad conversation—lots of praise, a little critique, advice, wishes for the story's direction, and random comments—folds into the creative process such that the line between writing a story and publishing it virtually disappears.[21]

While the social use of the site may reflect the development of contemporary participatory culture, the use of serials on Wattpad also evokes comparisons with the culture surrounding Victorian serials, as noted by Melanie Ramdarshan Bold:

> Like Dickens and his *Pickwick Papers*, Wattpad makes the creation of the book—the writing process—a collaboration between the author and the reader and is, in the words of Allen Lau, "disrupting the publishing industry" and also "disrupting the entertainment industry." . . . Writers can submit their book in a piecemeal way and receive feedback on each chapter or part: this not only allows the writer to understand what their reader wants but it helps to build up a readership and loyalty.[22]

Thus, in line with Wattpad's presentation of itself as, essentially, a social medium, both Bold and Vadde see the site as promoting a democratic literary culture, encouraging collaboration between readers and writers. Noting how the site disrupts the traditional hierarchical structures of the publishing system and the entertainment industry, Bold considers the site within the context of Jenkins' idea of a participatory turn and Johnson's concept of the citizen author as she suggests that the serial narratives on Wattpad promote a "grassroots" culture, allowing writers and readers to share their texts and interact with each other without being controlled by commercial interests.[23]

This idealistic image of Wattpad as a democratic space for literary engagement is supported by prominent users such as Margaret Atwood, who, as mentioned, emphasizes how Wattpad is free for everyone to use and argues that the site promotes young people's literacy. Atwood's Wattpad-novel, *The Happy Zombie Sunrise Home*, written together with Naomi Alderman, may be read accordingly as a reflection on the social uses of literature and the modes of intergenerational collaboration that are arguably promoted by the site. The novel uses the serial format to juxtapose chapters written from the perspectives of 18-year-old Okie (written by Alderman) and her grandmother Clio (written by Atwood). The story is set in a post-zombie-apocalypse world, drawing on (and humorously twisting) the popular young adult genre of zombie fiction.[24] After Okie's mother has turned into a zombie and consumed her father, Okie tries to reach the Canadian border to find safety with her grandmother in Toronto. The grandmother advises her, via mobile phone, about how to handle the situation, especially emphasizing the importance of books. As in *A Series of Unfortunate Events*, reading is presented as the road to salvation. While Okie is informed about the continuing significance of print literacy, the grandmother, in turn, learns to interpret Okie's cryptic text messages on the phone. Accordingly, both in its form and in its content, the novel may be read as a reflection on developing media literacies and intergenerational communication across media—quite in line with Atwood's argument that Wattpad promotes literary engagement in an age where many people express concerns about young people's declining literacy. Indeed, as the grandmother, Clio, states in the first chapter, the book is written everyone still in a "reading state"[25]—since the first symptom of people turning into zombies in the story is that they lose the ability to read. She concludes, directly addressing the Wattpad readers: "Let's just say that if you can read this, you're probably still unaffected."[26] In terms of the zombie apocalypse, the novel stages Wattpad as a "safe house" for literacy and literary culture as it encourages collaboration between different generations of "survivors"; people still in a "reading state" living in a post-apocalyptic modern world where the large majority of the population has turned into illiterate zombies.

The novel is written with much humor, but it does not escape a certain idealism, celebrating Wattpad as a new republic of letters, where generations meet up, and everyone is free to write and share their stories. However, Atwood and Alderman do not interact with their readers the way that most amateur writers on the site do, and they do not follow other Wattpad writers, except for each other. Their use of the site accordingly appears primarily as a statement, celebrating the democratic idea of the site without practically engaging in the Wattpad community. According to Melanie Ramdarshan Bold, this behavior among professional authors reflects how "instead of bringing consumers and celebrities together, and closing the power gap, social media actually illuminates the hierarchical divisions."[27] Accordingly, to further investigate the social use of the Wattpad site, it may be necessary to look more deeply into the "amateur" use of the site: How—originally— amateur authors and readers interact and communicate around serial narratives on Wattpad. Thus, I turn to the case of Anna Todd and her *After* series, one of the most famous successes in the site's history.

From Fan to Celebrity: Anna Todd's *After*

According to Wattpad's statistics, Anna Todd, with the Wattpad user profile "Imaginator1D," was, in 2018, the most read writer on the platform: with more followers and readers than such professional writers as Atwood or Paul Coelho.[28] Her popularity was especially triggered by the young adult romance novel *After*, which was written and published serially on Wattpad in 2016–2018, whereupon it landed a six-figure book deal with Simon & Schuster. Thus, Todd is an example of a Wattpad writer who entered the site as an amateur and used it to build an audience, ultimately allowing her to enter the traditional publishing system. In this way, she represents a new generation of authors, who, according to Bold, "are building audiences, on social platforms, through direct engagement with readers even before publishing through platforms such as Amazon/Kindle Direct."[29]

I will argue that Wattpad's serial publication model is central to how Todd uses the platform to build an audience and engage with this audience. That is, the *After* series exemplifies how the social aspects of serial publishing on Wattpad go hand in hand with a commercial purpose of generating interest and establishing a position within the traditional publishing system. Todd was already a successful writer within the Wattpad community before she wrote the *After* series, with 11 published stories on the platform. However, her real breakthrough was with *After*. *After* is categorized in Wattpad's romance section, and it is about the American girl Tessa, who begins attending college and falls in love with English "bad boy" Harry, as he is called in the original Wattpad version of the story. As suggested by Todd's Wattpad profile name, "Imaginator1D," the story is not only a romance but also fan fiction or a story belonging within the realm of fan culture: "Harry" refers to Harry Styles, the star in the popular boy band One Direction.[30] One Direction fan fiction is a dominant category on Wattpad, and originating within this community, *After* exemplifies how amateur fan writing on Wattpad may transit from fan culture to published writing and itself become an object of fan culture. However, before reaching traditional publication, *After* developed as an increasingly popular story on Wattpad. The love story of Tess and Harry is an illustrative case of serial narrativity, as it is dominated by a repetitive breaking-up-and-getting-back-together scheme that keeps the story going in three books or more than 300 chapters—illustrating Eco's argument that seriality is associated with repetition, disguised as variation.[31] Every time the series concludes in any kind of romantic harmony, somebody is hurt or betrayed, and Harry and Tess fight once again. In this way, the theme of what Tess and Todd's readers refer to as a "toxic" relationship allows Todd to avoid the common pitfalls in serial romantic fiction and tackle the challenge of moving beyond the "happy ever after."[32]

The serial aspect of the story is emphasized by the fact that Todd wrote the story on her mobile phone and published the chapters continually, as she wrote them. This routine of regular "updating," which is common among Wattpad users, is reflected in Todd's comments to the readers at the beginning of many chapters: "(If you all vote and comment like crazy, I will do a double update today, but since I write each chapter as I go, it won't be up until the evening:) xo),"[33] or "I decided to do a double update today, this chapter is shorter than usual but it is the second one for today so please don't complain that it is short."[34] These comments, written in the second book, after *After* developed into a popular phenomenon on the site, reflect how Todd directly communicates with her readers and encourages them to respond to her daily updates with comments and "votes"—even indicating that she will reward such responses with more updates. They suggest a culture in which there is much emphasis on quantitative feedback. Todd further notes, "Please please continue to vote and comment the way you are now! This is amazing. Ilysm!! xo."[35]

In this way, the logics of serial updating are used to secure regular, continuous attention from the fans, in terms of comments and votes, which will help spread the story to more Wattpad readers. According to Bronwen Thomas, the emphasis on feedback, in terms of quantitative numbers, generally characterizes amateur writing communities, especially fan fiction sites: "Fan fiction sites generally provide the user with information about the number of stories existing for each category, the number of reviews posted, and so on, conveying at a glance the sheer quantity of material that is available, as though that is some kind of guarantor of its quality."[36] Wattpad fits into this logic, as each chapter of any given story is presented with the number of reads, votes, and comments. In this way, the site reflects a "vote economy"—similar to Facebook's "like economy"—where value is measured in terms of the user's or reader's attention and votes, which may help the author get the book published by a traditional publisher and thus generate "real" commercial value.

Todd's regular, even daily, updates and her comments about these updates, their frequency, and when she will update again emphasize the social importance of seriality in the Wattpad publishing model. One reader, commenting on the text in Wattpad after the conclusion of the series, remembers how, "back in the day I used to msg all my friends when she would update"[37]— reflecting, almost nostalgically, on the time when the series was still running, and when readers had to wait, collectively, for new installments—whereas other readers express relief that the whole series is available and they do not have to wait. The social dimension in waiting for new chapters is emphasized by the authors' comments—for instance, Todd's claim that she would update once more that day if the readers would keep voting. This suggests how, in the Wattpad community, the social dimension of waiting and updating includes the author as well as the readers: As noted by Thomas, in relation to online fan communities, "The very fact of updating, and the fact that authors so frequently acknowledge the influence and support of others, suggests that a degree of mutual influence or dependency exists."[38] Moreover, Thomas concludes, "Intrinsic to the whole concept of updating is the idea of the work in progress."[39] Wattpad, as a site promoted especially for amateur authors, emphasizes this idea. The platform and the case of Todd's *After* reflect the concept of participatory culture where amateur writers post text to get feedback and thus further develop their work and skills.

However, in the case of Wattpad and the *After* series, especially, the participatory aspect is limited to the demand for new material, again emphasizing the serial aspect of the publishing process. Commenting on this fact as a general tendency within fan fiction communities, Thomas notes,

> The process of updating consists more of adding material, in the form of new chapters, rather than necessarily revising already existing material. In this respect, the process has clear parallels with the serialization of novels in the nineteenth century, or contemporary televised soap operas, where anticipation and discussion of coming plotlines and developments are intrinsic to the narrative experience.[40]

Todd's comments exemplify this tendency as she focuses primarily on uploading more chapters, expanding the story. Thomas further elaborates on the significance of updating in fan communities, noting that "updating helps to fulfil . . . the 'desire for the inexhaustible story' . . . . The vehemence of the fans' exhortations to authors to keep updating is testament to this, and most reviews actually consist primarily of exhortations to 'keep going' or to 'update soon,' usually accompanied by the inevitable excess of expressive punctuation."[41] The comments posted on Wattpad in relation to the *After* series, when the series was still running, reflect this tendency, and these comments are furthermore paralleled by the author's continuing encouragements to "keep voting and commenting" (usually followed by her equally excessive use of expressive punctuation).

The *After* series thus reflect a participatory culture that is focused on the concept of serial *continuation*, as reflected in the activity of updating, and in the repeated encouragements from both readers and author to continue voting and updating, respectively. Regular updates become the center of social interaction that goes beyond mere discussion of and communication about the text. That is, Todd uses the daily updates to communicate with her readers in a way that suggests a friendly, even personal approach: For instance, in one chapter introduction, she writes a birthday wish to a specific reader: suggesting that she even communicates privately with some of her readers. The birthday wish led to a long thread of comments where people write when they have their birthday.[42] At first glance, this thread appears as a rather meaningless form of communication that does not have much to do with the text. As such, however, it does illustrate the large amount of so-called "phatic" communication in online reading communities, communication merely or primarily for the sake of communication.[43] In Chapter 2, I described a similar tendency in the *Familiar* reading club on Facebook, with readers (and the author) sharing images of their cats and catching up on each other rather than, merely, discussing the novel. Thomas accordingly notes how fan sites are "as much for social networking as they are for the expression and sharing of esthetic evaluations"[44] and, as a platform targeted toward young writers, the social aspect of the Wattpad platform is central, if not dominant.

Through her personal messages and direct comments to selected readers, Todd encourages this primarily social use of the site. Contrary to Atwood and Alderman, who act as professional authors, let the text speak for itself, and do not interact personally with the readers, Tood clearly identifies as a part of the Wattpad community. As indicated by her profile name, Imaginator1D, she also identifies as a fan and a part of the One Direction community. Accordingly, her case may, at first glance, reflect the participatory aspect of the Wattpad site that is celebrated by Atwood, where the boundaries between authors and writers and between amateurs and professionals are blurring. However, as the *After* series develops and gains in popularity, Todd's status within the Wattpad community changes, as do the social dynamics surrounding the series. Bold thus, in 2018, categorizes Todd as a "micro-celebrity." Within the Wattpad community, Bold explains, micro-celebrities "view their followers as a fan base, rather than friends, so it creates a relationship of power. This unequal relationship is recognized by both micro-celebrity and follower, with the fans behaving deferentially."[45] The fans' comments are primarily celebratory and encouraging in relation to this category of authors: As noted earlier, the participatory aspect is, more or less, reduced to readers' encouragements for Todd to "go on" and "keep updating." An element of actual revision or rewriting of the series is introduced in the process leading toward publication, but only after the conclusion of the series, when Todd herself rewrites the series prior to publishing it with Simon & Schuster. For instance, she changes the names of the characters in the story so that it no longer appears as a One Direction fan fiction. However, this latter process of rewriting appears to have been initiated by the commercial publisher to avoid legal consequences referring to the band and Harry Styles, rather than in response to the readers' feedback.

As a result, the series progressed from fan fiction to a bestselling published novel. Todd moved from one realm to another. She departed from the realm of fan culture, where her series was also evaluated by fans and praised as a fan fiction: Many early readers, for instance, comment how they value hints to the One Direction group and specific songs. However, the One Direction connection becomes less significant as the series is published and develops a fan community of its own. Many Wattpad readers begin to present themselves as "rereaders," as opposed to the "newcomers" to the series and thus contribute to producing an idea of the series as an object to celebrate in itself—while also demonstrating decreasing awareness of the work as a piece of fan culture. This tendency creates a tension, which is documented in the comments on Wattpad, between those readers, who recognize the book as a One Direction fan fiction, and those who perceive it otherwise—possibly because they read the new version, where "Harry" is turned into "Hardin." The latter readers often express disbelief and even disappointment when they realize that it is originally fan fiction—suggesting that this kind of literature is perceived as less valuable and original than other works.

Whereas Atwood and Alderman write on Wattpad as professionals and remain above their readers in the literary hierarchy, Todd is interesting as an author who uses Wattpad to balance between different positions on a platform and in a culture, where the boundaries between author and reader, or fan, are blurred. Her journey as an author culminates with the Simon & Schuster publication of the *After* series and its adaptation into a movie: Topics that become quite dominant on Wattpad when both newcomers and rereaders report comparing the original Wattpad series to the published books and the film. Todd's case accordingly illustrates the commercial potential of the Wattpad site: Rather than merely promoting a free and democratic exchange of texts and feedback, the site also functions as a way to help authors move toward traditional commercial publication. Bold notes,

> There are numerous threads, in the different Wattpad clubs, dedicated to advice and tips on securing a traditional publisher. Additionally, just under a quarter (37%) [sic!] of the authors, including the verified authors, have been or are in the process of being traditionally published and nearly half of these have been or will be published as a result of being on Wattpad.[46]

In this context, Wattpad's serial format functions similarly to the feuilleton format of 19th-century novels: The initial serial publication for free or, in the case of the historical feuilletons, in cheap pamphlets, promotes social interaction around the work and thus helps build an audience for the work or the author, paving the way for a more finite and lasting publication as a bound book.

Conclusion: Social and Commercial Seriality on Wattpad

The two Wattpad novels discussed earlier represent different uses of the serial publishing model on Wattpad. Atwood and Alderman's zombie novel reflects how established authors use the platform in a somewhat idealistic way to share their work and celebrate the democratic and collaborative potential of social media culture: Yet they do not themselves interact with their readers and the participatory aspect is, accordingly, limited; the hierarchies remain. Anna Todd, on the other hand, embraces the Wattpad community—her work itself emerges as a piece of fan fiction, embedded in a fan culture based on Wattpad. She uses the serial format to engage and communicate continually with her readers in the context of each update, thus increasing her work's popularity, its number of "reads" and "votes," and developing fan fiction into a published work.

Despite these differences, both cases reflect how the social and participatory aspects of the Wattpad community are connected to the economic incentives of serial publishing on Wattpad. Accordingly, my analyses complicate the site's image as a space of free, democratic participation. Certainly, Wattpad's serial publishing format serves not only to encourage social interaction and a free flow of feedback and ideas, but this very social interaction is also used to promote the site and the stories and increase their chances of success beyond the site. In this way, both professional authors and amateurs arguably use the serial format in the same way as Storytel, discussed in chapter five, namely, to promote user loyalty. The case of Wattpad in this way reflects how the format is used to produce commercial value on a free site that functions according to the logics of sharing and participation, dominant in digital culture. This commercial potential in the serial format is emphasized by the fact that Wattpad inserts advertisements in between chapters of the most popular texts, including *After*, making the readers watch if they want to keep reading—presenting the literary equivalent of the commercial break in television.[47] This commercial use of the serial format must be considered in the context of Wattpad's overall business model, as described by Rosamund Davies: "As a commercial enterprise, Wattpad's business model is, like that of many other digital networks, to monetize its community by selling its attention, its data and also its creative services to other businesses."[48] These "other businesses" may be commercial advertisers, but it may also be professional or self-publishing authors, using the site to build a readership for their novels. Furthermore, Wattpad writers also contribute to creating attention around specific brands or artists through the extensive production of fan fiction on the site. Not least, the commercial incentives for authors using the site rely on the fact that it functions as a gateway to publication with traditional publishers—with *After* as one of the most prominent examples.[49] Popular Wattpad authors are interesting for publishers because they bring along a loyal readership from the platform. Obviously, only a small percentage of the Wattpad writers manage to get published by traditional publishers, but the mere possibility adds to the commercial value of the site.

The case of serial publishing and reading on Wattpad in this way illustrates the connection between the social aspects and the commercial uses of serialization in contemporary literary digital culture. Digital serialization functions as a commercial strategy to promote old and new literary works, exactly because it is also a social strategy, following the logics of sharing and participation which dominate digital culture. The site may be connected to broader developments toward a participatory culture as described by Jenkins, an emphasis on the process rather than the product and on the productive collaboration between readers and authors. The fact that a large part of the stories published on Wattpad belongs to the category of fan fiction emphasizes this aspect, suggesting how readers, or fans, become writers. Indeed, the genre of fan fiction may be considered in relation to serialization as a mode of continuing the existing work or product. While Jenkins, along with professional Wattpad users such as Margaret Atwood, celebrates the possibilities implied by digital publishing to move toward a democratic culture of sharing, rather than selling, stories, I have demonstrated how the social uses of the serial format are deeply connected to the commercial aspect—because social engagement generates commercial value in a digital culture. Wattpad uses the serial format to promote readers' social investment in the stories, attracting the users' attention which may then be used commercially—for instance, by advertisers, filling out the commercial breaks between chapters, by publishers to spot new talents, or by professional or self-published authors, promoting their works in serial format via the platform.

Furthermore, Wattpad, similarly to Storytel, uses the serial format to present stories in a way that is fit for mobile reading—in small bits, quickly read on the smartphone. In the case of Wattpad, even the writing process is often mobile. Reportedly, 85% of Wattpad users are reading and writing via mobile devices.[50] The serial narratives on Wattpad thus bear witness to the way in which shifting medial as well as social and commercial contexts shapes contemporary literary texts. First and foremost, the case of Wattpad illustrates how the current resurgence of serial publishing may be connected to the process of digitalization and the commercial as well as social logics of digital culture.

However, the most successful series on Wattpad are also published as printed books—just like the most popular Storytel Originals series. Listing the benefits of publishing with Wattpad, Wattpad's guidelines emphasize the possibility of being discovered by traditional publishers, highlighting the stories of published Wattpad authors such as Anna Todd. The publication of *After*, similarly to the paperback publications of *Virus* and other born-audio series, accordingly, suggests the continuing significance of traditional literary institutions: In these cases, digital serialization is a part of a process, which may lead to discovery, commercial success, and final publication in printed book format—just as was the case with the feuilleton novels by Dickens or Dumas. Again, we may stress the continuing relevance of the printed book, as also discussed in relation to *The Familiar*. Whether or not the literary system will keep functioning like this in an increasingly digitized culture remains to be seen, just as it remains to be seen whether or not the printed book format will remain the end goal of the serialization process—so, it seems proper to conclude this final chapter with a "to be continued . . ."

Notes

1. Margaret Atwood, "Why Wattpad Works," *The Guardian,* July 6, 2012, www.theguardian.com/books/2012/jul/06/margaret-atwood-wattpad-online-writing.
2. Ibid.
3. Henry Jenkins, *Convergence Culture. Where Old and New Media Collide* (New York and London: New York University Press, 2006); Claire Squires and Padmini Ray Murray, "The Digital Publishing Communications Circuit," *Book 2.0* 3, no. 1 (2013): 3–23.
4. Squires and Murray, "Circuit," 17–18.
5. Henry Jenkins, "The Cultural Logic of Media Convergence," *International Journal of Cultural Studies* 7, no. 1 (2004): 37–38.
6. Miriam Johnson, "The Rise of the Citizen Author. Writing Within Social Media," *Publishing Research Quarterly* 33, no. 2 (2017): 131–46.
7. Aarthi Vadde, "Amateur Creativity. Contemporary Literature and the Digital Publishing Scene," *New Literary History* 48 (2017): 27–51.
8. Jennifer Poole Hayward, *Consuming Pleasures: Active Audiences and Serial Fictions from Dickens to Soap Opera* (Lexington: University Press of Kentucky, 1997).
9. Frank Kelleter, "Five Ways of Looking at Popular Seriality," in *Media of Serial Narratives,* ed. Frank Kelleter (Columbus: The Ohio State University Press, 2017), 13.
10. Ibid., 14.
11. Vadde, "Amateur," 24.
12. Monica Miller, "What Wattpad Brings to the Publishing Table," *PUB 800,* December 9, 2015, https://tkbr.publishing.sfu.ca/pub800/2015/12/what-wattpad-brings-to-the-table/.
13. According to Wattpad's numbers, presented on https://company.wattpad.com.
14. Vadde, "Amateur," 28.
15. Wattpad FAQ, www.wattpad.com/writers/faq/.
16. "Should I post my whole novel all at once or serialize it," Wattpad user forum, anonymous user, www.wattpadwriters.com/t/should-i-post-my-whole-novel-all-at-once-or-serialize-it/99503.

17. Wattpad, "Should I," anonymous user.
18. Melanie Ramdarshan Bold, "The Return of the Social Author: Negotiating Authority and Influence on Wattpad," *Convergence* 24, no. 2 (2018): 124–25.
19. Wattpad FAQ.
20. This use of the site may be compared to the promotional use of serialized Twitter fiction, as examined by Tore Rye Andersen in relation to David Mitchell's "@I_Bombadil." Andersen points out how Mitchell published the story on Twitter in order to create buzz and recruit loyal readers for his forthcoming novel. See Tore Rye Andersen, "Staggered Transmissions: Twitter and the Return of Serialized Literature," *Convergence* 23, no. 1 (2017): 34–48.
21. Vadde, "Amateur," 37.
22. Bold, "Social Author," 124–25.
23. Ibid.
24. The novel's zombie-motif may be discussed in relation to Alderman's background as the author of the app, *Zombies, Run*. The app combines the affordances of the audiobook and the interactive game, encouraging a mobile and interactive listening experience as it integrates a story about zombie attacks into the user's daily activities such as running. While the app thus exemplifies an individualized use of the digitally distributed story, Atwood and Alderman's Wattpad novel emphasizes the social aspects of consuming literature and surviving zombies.
25. Margaret Atwood and Naomi Alderman, *The Happy Zombie Sunrise Home* (Wattpad, 2013), www.wattpad.com/8283993-the-happy-zombie-sunrise-home-chapter-1-clio.
26. Ibid.
27. Bold, "Social Author," 128.
28. Ibid.
29. Ibid., 119.
30. In the published print version, all references that identify the text as a fan fiction have been removed, and Harry is renamed Harkin.
31. Umberto Eco, *The Limits of Interpretation* (Bloomington and Indianapolis: Indiana University Press, 1991).
32. For a discussion of this problem in romantic serial fiction, see An Goris, "Happily Ever After . . . and After: Serialization and the Popular Romance Novel," *Americana* 12 no. 1 (2013), www.americanpopularculture.com/journal/articles/spring_2013/goris.htm.
33. Anna Todd, *After 2*. Wattpad, 2017. Author's note to chapter 115.
34. Todd, *After 2*. Author's note to chapter 122.
35. Todd, *After 2*. Author's note to Chapter 134.
36. Bronwen Thomas, "Update Soon! Harry Potter Fanfiction and Narrative as a Participatory Process," in *New Narratives: Stories and Storytelling in the Digital Age,* eds. Ruth Page and Bronwen Thomas (Lincoln: University of Nebraska Press, 2011), 215.
37. Anonymous Wattpad user, responding to *After*.
38. Thomas, "Update," 213.
39. Ibid., 214.
40. Ibid., 213.
41. Ibid., 215.
42. The serial updating format generally draws attention to dates and temporality: A similar example is the long commenting threads that occur in the ending of the

After books, where people write the specific date when they finished reading the series, resulting in a kind of celebratory atmosphere, as people socialize about having finished the book.
43. On phatic communication in fan cultures, see Tore Rye Andersen and Sara Tanderup Linkis, "As We Speak. Concurrent Narration and Participation in the digitally distributed serial narratives *Skam* and @I_Bombadil," *Narrative* 27, no. 1 (2019): 83–106.
44. Thomas, "Update," 211.
45. Bold, "Social Author," 119.
46. Ibid., 122.
47. If you want to avoid these in-text commercials, you will have to update to a paid "premium" Wattpad membership—again stressing the commercial aspect of the site.
48. Rosamund Davies, "Collaborative Production and the Transformation of Publishing: The Case of Wattpad," in *Collaborative Production in the Creative Industries,* eds. J. Graham J and A. Gandini (London: University of Westminster Press, 2017), 60.
49. Wattpad notably helped Todd land her deal with Simon & Schuster, see Madison Malone Kirscher, "This Woman Wrote Fan-Fic on Her Phone and Ended Up with a Major Book Deal," *Business Insider,* July 28, 2015, www.businessinsider.com/anna-todd-earns-book-and-movie-deals-for-one-direction-fanfiction-2015-7?r=UK&IR=T—a story which suggests the site's active role and interest in promoting the users' texts.
50. Miller, "What Wattpad Brings."

7 Conclusion

In 2018, Danielewski's *The Familiar* was paused by Pantheon due to declining sales. By 2021, Storytel has more or less abandoned the episodic format as most of their original productions—while still labeled as serials—are no longer published in separate episodes. Both cases reflect attempts to import the serial format, primarily associated with television series, into literary culture, across media and markets. Neither experiment really succeeded, at least not from the publishers' perspectives. *The Familiar* did not attract enough readers to justify its expensive layout and the monumental scale of the project. Also, Storytel's listeners would more often jump off the series in between episodes than be encouraged by the format to keep listening. Thus, it is tempting to consider the two cases as illustrations of Roger Hagedorn's observation that the serial format is "a consistent loser."[1] Historically and in contemporary media culture, the format has been used to market books and attract attention from the media and potential consumers, but in the long run—Hagedorn, of course, speaks in terms of media history—it is often abandoned.

Yet, as I have argued in this book, the story about the serial resurgence in contemporary literature is more complex than that. Rather than a consistent loser, the series has proved successful when it comes to narrative innovation and development of storyworlds across volumes and media, as illustrated by the series by Snicket and Pullman, and when it comes to reinventing publishing in the digital age, for instance, as reflected in the use of the serial format on Wattpad. While the goal of many Wattpad writers may be to publish a finite, printed book, online publication in serial format is an important step toward that end. Thus, focusing on serialization does not necessarily mean focusing on the end goal or the ending of a story: Endings are indeed often problematic in series, as Lemony Snicket reminds us. Rather, as reflected by the cases of Wattpad and Storytel, serialization may be part of the beginning—of introducing a new medium, a new format, or a new author.

DOI: 10.4324/9781003265894-7

Not least, focusing on serialization means an emphasis on the process. As demonstrated in my analyses in this book, it means exploring how narrative content is continuously influenced by medial, social, and economic contexts. Later, I discuss my results regarding this process, focusing on the different but interrelated perspectives that were outlined in my introduction: The narrative, medial, and the social and economic aspects of serialization in literary culture.

Narrative Aspects: Complex Worlds—and Simple Stories

Serial narratives are traditionally defined by repetition and regularity, as emphasized by both Umberto Eco and Hagedorn.[2] Complicating this classic definition, I have invoked Jason Mittell's concept of narrative complexity in modern television series. He argues that this feature is specific for television series, noting, for instance, that new conditions for producing and distributing television series in the digital age allow for longer, more complex narratives.[3] However, as I have demonstrated, a development toward narrative complexity can be seen in serial literature as well, partly but not exclusively because many literary works are inspired by modern television series. Danielewski's *The Familiar* is an obvious example. Here, the sheer monumentality of the serial project, along with a multi-layered narrative structure and multimodal experiments, is used to complicate the story of a little girl who finds a cat. Serialization, here, is associated with duration, and with the ambition of telling a story with a "different kind of pace"[4]—the pacing that Danielewski associates with modern television series. Thus, as a work that takes time, to write and to read, and with a timeline that spans from prehistoric times and far into the future, the series aims at producing "a sense of time that exceeds a decade."[5]

Mittell describes how, in contemporary series, the established distinction between the "episodic" format and continuous "serial" narratives is complicated. Lemony Snicket's *A Series of Unfortunate Events* evolves from a repetitive, episodic format toward a more complex structure as the story unfolds across volumes—and as the protagonists grow older and grow up. A similar development toward greater narrative complexity, aligned with the process of maturation of the protagonists and the (implied) readers, can also be observed in Pulman's *His Dark Materials* and related materials. In Chapter 4, I argued that the development toward increasing serial complexity may here be connected to the concept of the serial storyworld.[6] Focusing on the series as a "world": A space to traverse and engage in indeed makes it possible to consider how this space is gradually expanded—and complicated—as characters and readers become increasingly mature and as the story unfolds across different volumes and media.

It is thus possible to point to development toward narrative complexity in contemporary serial literature. It is, however, also worth noting that Eco's concept of the repetitive series is still relevant and dominant in the world of popular serial storytelling. Anna Todd's Wattpad novel *After*, discussed in Chapter 6, may exemplify such a story, focusing on a repetitive falling-in-love-and-breaking-up scheme, as may many Storytel Originals, where plot curves and cliffhangers are—almost—defined by a recipe and produced by algorithms. However, the fact that Storytel, responding to listener response, adjusted their use of the format and returned to a more traditional literary format—the 9–10-hour novel—reflects what Mark Turner calls the "unruliness" of serial narratives.[7] Writing about Victorian novels, Turner points out how even these, now canonical, texts were often paused or developed in different ways than planned when published in their original feuilleton format. Far from being defined, merely, by narrative repetition, predictability, and regularity, serial narratives are subject to external factors, such as unpredictable listener behavior, changing economic conditions, or the outbreak of a pandemic, which may influence the conditions for production and distribution, and reception—as well as the narrative content of the series. The case of Storytel, abandoning the episodic format, exemplifies the unruliness of contemporary serial production, as does Danielewski's paused project, or, for that matter, the immense success of Todd's Wattpad novel. Thus, the narrative development of serial texts should be considered in relation to the medial, social, and economic dimensions of serialization.

Medial Aspects: Transmediality and Medium Specificity

The tendencies described earlier regarding the narrative content in contemporary series are closely related to the medial aspects and specifically to the concept of serialization as a transmedial phenomenon. Most of the cases discussed in the book reflect how series are developed across media or as a result of intermedial exchange. Most dominant among my selected cases is the influence from television series: Danielewski's novel may be described as a remediation of modern complex television series, while the television adaptations of the works by Snicket and Pullman arguably contribute to their narrative complexity and worldbuilding. Accordingly, complicating Jason Mittell's concept of serial complexity, which is specific for the television series, I have introduced the concept of *transmedia complexity*: Addressing the idea that the narrative content and serial structure are complicated as the series is developed across media and formats.

This development may be related to the concept of transmedia storytelling, as promoted by Henry Jenkins, and transmedial worlds, introduced by

Marie-Laure Ryan.[8] As narratology's traditional emphasis on "narratives" is replaced by an orientation toward "worlds," it becomes possible to consider how different media products and versions contribute to the aspect of worldbuilding. This also means that we move away from established hierarchical relations between media formats. Television series may inspire novels, as well as vice versa, and book series may supplement and develop a story originally presented in a television series. The television adaptations of the works by Pullman and Snicket illustrate this tendency as they contribute to developing and complicating the stories from the books: HBO's version of *His Dark Materials* combines perspectives from different volumes and book series, and the Netflix adaptation of *A Series of Unfortunate Events* not only departs from the storyline from the book but also makes a point of it to the extent that one of the characters cries out: "It's off-book!"

This development toward serial transmediality in literature may be considered as an aspect of modern convergence culture, as discussed by Jenkins, or in relation to Jim Collins' argument that literary culture is turning into popular culture.[9] Collins sees the tendency of contemporary television series overtaking the status of literature and becoming the "new novels" as an indication that serial narratives are no longer medium specific.[10] However, I oppose that idea, hence the emphasis in the book on serialization in *literary* culture. While the logics of other media, such as television, podcasts, or social media may influence literature, it is also an art form in its own right. This book has explored what happens to that art form as literary serials develop across media and markets. Several of my analyses accordingly emphasize the significance of medium specificity. While imitating television series, Danielewski's *The Familiar* develops the serial format according to the affordances of the printed book, performing bookish seriality—whereas Storytel's Originals have been adjusted specifically for the digital audiobook and its intended audience. The format, the medium, and the materiality of both do matter, and the feedback loops between different media, illustrated by the analyses presented in this book, reflect how literary serial narratives are developed in a fine balance between transmediality and medium specificity.

Social and Economic Aspects: Serial Participation and Commercialization

The developments described earlier toward narrative complexity, serial worldbuilding, and transmedial storytelling go hand in hand with developments in how we use serial narratives. Jenkins explicitly links modern convergence culture and transmedia storytelling to participatory culture. According to him, serial audiences are encouraged to participate and engage in the unfolding transmedial storyworld as they are moving between different media and versions.[11] Furthermore, an emphasis on storyworlds suggests that, rather than merely consuming stories, audiences are expected to enter the narrative world and engage in all aspects of it, watching the movie, playing the game, making connections between different versions, and buying extra material and new editions.

Jenkins links this development explicitly to modern culture and traces it back to the active fan communities surrounding television and film series in the 20th century. However, by focusing on serialization, it becomes possible to emphasize an aspect of historical continuity in relation to participatory culture. Serial literature has always been surrounded by engaged audiences, and the Facebook groups celebrating Danielewski's works, or the listener communities surrounding Storytel's series, may thus be considered in relation to the reading cultures surrounding the works of Dickens, Flaubert, or Dumas. Yet, while serialization has always been associated with participation and active readers, digitalization and new media mean that the possibilities for participation have changed dramatically in recent years. Social media make it easier for readers or users to discuss series in-between episodes or volumes, as is the case with both the *Familiar* and the Storytel reading groups, and it becomes possible to influence the story in new ways as authors and publishers are often present on these media forums as well. Claire Squires and Padmini Ray Murray noted that the digital literary culture turns readers into prosumers and co-promoters who contribute to producing and promoting books, using social media, blogs, or review functions on Amazon or in the Storytel app.[12] These developments become even more evident when it comes to serial production since, when a story is developed and published serially, it becomes possible to comment and influence its future development. Wattpad most clearly exemplifies the participatory aspect of digitalized serial culture as writers and readers share parts of stories to be developed collaboratively. As discussed in Chapter 6, the site may be considered to embody the democratic potential of digital literary culture, following Jenkins and Aarthi Vadde[13]: A culture where everybody can participate and where professional authors write alongside aspiring amateurs—as indicated in Atwood and Alderman's zombie novel focusing on intergenerational collaboration.

However, these democratic ideas may also be questioned. Far from all readers or authors take part in participatory culture. Furthermore, the participatory aspect of serial culture is linked directly to the commercial aspect—serialization as a business strategy. Frank Kelleter notes that the serial format is, in essence, a capitalist form—produced to generate demand for "more of the same." While this might not be true of all forms of serial storytelling, this logic does become apparent in relation to several of the cases investigated in this book. Serialization on Wattpad, for instance, is often used as a strategy to attract "reads" and promote the stories, a development which will ultimately lead to profitable publication, with Anna Todd's *After* series as an obvious example. Furthermore, the tendencies toward transmedial development, discussed in relation to the Snicket and Pullman series, may not only contribute to building narrative complexity, but they also reflect commercialization of the story—as Snicket himself ironically muses in his letter announcing the Netflix adaptation of *A Series of Unfortunate Events*. Series become franchises, an aspect which is also visible in Danielewski's attempts to sell merchandise. Again, this is not a new development. As noted in my introduction, serialization was always closely associated with economic incentives: The series as a literary format originated as an attempt to sell newspapers and journals. The commercial potential of the serial format is also reflected by the fact that most bestselling novels are parts of series, as noted by Ann Steiner. According to her, serialization, along with a potential for transmedial development, increases a book's chance of commercial success.[14] The Snicket and Pullman series, discussed in this study, exemplify this logic.

While the commercial use of the serial format is nothing new, digital distribution models put new emphasis on serialization as a business model. Storytel's use of the serial format illustrates this tendency. The subscription-based model of the streaming service means that it becomes important not only to sell books but also to make readers keep reading, or listening, month after month, and one way to do this is to produce series that readers want to return to season after season.[15] Furthermore, as discussed by Karl Berglund and Ann Steiner, the serial format helps consumers navigate in the vast amount of accessible titles on the streaming service. Every time a new installment appears, new interest is sparked in the previous installments and thus in the services' backlist catalog.[16] Åberg's *Virus* series is an obvious example of this tendency, as the series was developed in seven seasons, resulting in one of the most successful Storytel Originals series in Sweden. The fact that the success of this series was possibly fueled by the Covid-19 pandemic in 2020/2021 once again reflects the unruliness of contemporary serial publications.

Something to Return to? Post-Pandemic Seriality

Most of the research presented in this book was conducted in 2018–2020 as a part of the research project, "Serialization in Contemporary Literature and Culture"; however, the book was finished in spring 2021 as the world and this author was recovering after a year of crisis caused by the Covid-19 pandemic. Like most crises, the pandemic threw new light on everyday life

Conclusion 109

and death as well as on the research subject, and I accordingly want to conclude with a few reflections on the "post-pandemic" significance of series and serialization in contemporary literature and culture.

Crises are not bad for everybody. It was not only Åberg's *Virus* series, which most likely benefitted from increasing attention due to the pandemic. Streaming services in general, including services for e-books and audiobooks, experienced great success in 2020.[17] Thus, in Scandinavia, digital book sales increased dramatically—in Sweden, an important threshold was passed as, for the first time, digital books made up more than half (57%) of all volumes sold on the Swedish book market.[18] Exactly why this development concurred with the pandemic, and if there is a connection between the two events, remains to be examined, but one can speculate that lockdowns, isolation at home, and limited access to physical stores encouraged people to consume books in digital formats. How serialization fits into this development may also be worth exploring. As I discuss elsewhere, serial narratives in digital formats fit well into modern everyday life and daily routines.[19] A 50-minute episode of an audiobook feuilleton or a chapter of the favorite series on Wattpad can easily be combined with the daily commute, breakfast rituals, or exercising. However, for most people, these routines were disrupted by the pandemic and the general demand to work—and stay, and live—at home to prevent the virus from spreading. Storytel reacted promptly by adjusting their book recommendations to this new situation. For instance, the Danish version of the Storytel app recommended books on viruses, and a new category appeared in the app: "Long books for the lockdown." Furthermore, several new audiobook productions directly addressed the new situation, including the Originals series "Dagbok från Coronabubblan" ("Diary from the Corona bubble") by the Swedish journalist Cecilia Garme. In the series, Garme, in 10–15-minute episodes, presents a day-to-day account of the events during the outbreak of the virus in Sweden in the spring of 2020. Garme presents the diary as an attempt to capture how the virus transformed everyday life, and while she does mention public events related to the virus outbreak in Sweden, her emphasis is on her transformed daily life and her experience of isolation at home. This intimate perspective is stressed by the fact that the audiobook was recorded in an improvised home studio in her closet.[20]

The "corona diary" reflects how, in a time of crisis, we may return to some of the old functions of literary series as theorized by Eco: The series is associated with repetition, stability, and familiarity. Garme's series, with its short episodes focusing on everyday life, is designed to function as a daily reference point during the crisis. Several comments by users in the Storytel app reflect that the series does, indeed, function in this way: Listeners report that they listen to the diary on a daily basis and appreciate the sense of recognizability and communality that it provides, the feeling that "we are all in the same boat"—hence, the series is associated with a social aspect.[21] My personal pandemic experience supports this connection. In my family—with two boys, age 8 and 11—the lockdown periods became associated with systematic consumption of film and television series, including all Marvel Avengers and Star Wars films—an inclination which can be linked to Disney's strategic launch of the streaming service Disney+, with access to all this content, during the pandemic winter of 2020–2021. While expensive—the film nights have, of course, been followed by the purchase of various Avengers and Star Wars merchandise—the shared experience of returning to these serial universes, night after night, provided a sense of stability, predictability, and familiarity in a situation otherwise characterized by uncertainly caused by the virus outbreak and dominated by daily updates on the numbers of people infected and dead.

What can these (admittedly anecdotal) examples of the uses of serial narratives during a crisis tell us? The serial format, as a form of publication, may indeed be unruly and unpredictable, as argued by Turner, yet series are also associated with regularity, repetition, and familiarity, as emphasized by Eco. First and foremost, this book has presented a view on serial narratives that complicate Eco's ideas by focusing on the development of contemporary literary serials across media and markets. I have explored the narrative, medial, social, and commercial aspects of serialization, and I have highlighted the links between these aspects. Thus, I have connected development toward greater narrative complexity, following Mittell, to tendencies toward transmedia storytelling and worldbuilding, introduced by Jenkins and Ryan. These aspects are again associated with new forms of serial engagement and participation; tendencies which, in turn, may be linked to broader developments in modern media culture where the boundaries between producers and consumers are blurred, and where users turn into co-promoters and prosumers. These tendencies are again associated with new (and old) uses of the serial as a business model. Certainly, all of these developments reflect a tendency where literature is further integrated into modern media culture, as perhaps most clearly reflected by the cases of Wattpad and Storytel, which distribute stories quite the same way as other platforms distribute films, television series, or video clips.

Yet, as I have argued, the cases explored also, in different ways, relate to serialization as cultural practice in literary history. As my personal experience during the pandemic reflects, the format does, indeed, still function similarly to Dickens's feuilleton novels—producing social engagement and a demand for more. Far from being a "consistent loser," the serial format has proved an effective format during the recent crisis: It is something to return to, even when the world is on fire. Modern inventions—such as the transformations in publishing caused by digitalization—appear only to strengthen the format further. As the examples of Wattpad and Storytel reflect, new publishing models increasingly turn to the format to secure success. Thus, while serial narratives have been present in literary culture for centuries, new media and tendencies in the book market will, most likely, only make the format more central for storytelling in the future.

Notes

1. Roger Hagedorn, "Technology and Economic Exploitation: The Serial as a Form of Narrative Presentation," *Wide Angle* 10, no. 4 (1988): 5.
2. Umberto Eco, *The Limits of Interpretation* (Bloomington and Indianapolis: Indiana University Press, 1990): Hagedorn, "Technology."
3. Jason Mittell, *Complex TV. The Poetics of Contemporary Television Storytelling* (New York: New York University Press, 2015).
4. Mark Z. Danielewski, "The Rumpus Interview with Mark Danielewski," interview by Dylan Foley, *The Rumpus*, May 20, 2015, https://therumpus.net/2015/05/the-rumpus-interview-with-mark-danielewski/.
5. Mark Z. Danielewski, "A Conversation With Mark Z. Danielewski," interview by Philbert Dy, *Rogue Books*, 2017, http://rogue.ph/conversation-mark-z-danielewski/.
6. Marie-Laure Ryan, "Story/World/Media. Turning the Instruments of a Media-Conscious Narratology," in *Storyworlds Across Media. Toward a Media-Conscious Narratology*, eds. Marie-Laure Ryan and Jan-Noël Thon (Lincoln and London: University of Nebraska Press, 2014), 33.
7. Mark W. Turner, "The Unruliness of Serials in the Nineteenth Century (and in the Digital Age)," in *Serialization in Popular Culture*, eds. Rob Allen and Thijs van den Berg (New York: Routledge, 2014), 11–31.
8. Marie-Laure Ryan and Jan-Noël Thon, eds., *Storyworlds Across Media. Toward a Media-Conscious Narratology* (Lincoln and London: University of Nebraska Press, 2014).
9. Jim Collins, *Bring on the Books for Everybody* (Durham and London: Duke University Press), 2010.
10. Jim Collins, "Fifty Shades of Seriality and E-Readers Games," *Akademisk Kvarter* 7 (2013): 374–75.
11. Henry Jenkins, *Convergence Culture. Where Old and New Media Collide* (New York and London: New York University Press, 2006).
12. Claire Squires and Padmini Ray Murray, "The Digital Publishing Communications Circuit," *Book 2.0* 3, no. 1 (2013): 3–23.
13. Jenkins, *Convergence*; Aarthi Vadde, "Amateur Creativity. Contemporary Literature and the Digital Publishing Scene," *New Literary History* 48 (2017): 27–51.
14. Ann Steiner, "Serendipity, Promotion, and Literature," in *Hype. Bestsellers and Literary Culture*, eds. Jon Helgason, Sara Kärrholm and Ann Steiner (Lund: Nordic Academic Press, 2014), 45.
15. See Sara Tanderup Linkis and Julia Pennlert, "Episodic Listening: Analysing the Usage and Content of Born-Audio Serials," *Journal of Electronic Publishing* 20, no. 3 (2021), https://doi.org/10.3998/3336451.0023.102.

16. Karl Berglund and Ann Steiner, "Is Backlist the New Frontlist," *Logos* 32, no. 1 (2021): 14.
17. On the general success of streaming services during the pandemic, see Lillian Rizzo and Drew Fitzgerald, "Forget the Streaming Wars—Pandemic-Stricken 2020 Lifted Netflix and Others," *Wall Street Journal*, December 30, 2020, www.wsj.com/articles/forget-the-streaming-warspandemic-stricken-2020-lifted-netflix-and-others-11609338780. On Storytel's growth in 2020, see Storytel, "Annual Report and Sustainability Report," https://investors.storytel.com/en/wp-content/uploads/sites/2/2021/04/storytel-annual-report-2020-storytel-ab-publ-210401.pdf.
18. Erik Wikberg, *Bokförsäljningsstatistiken: Helåret 2020* (Stockholm: Svenska Förläggareföreningen, 2021), 23–24. A similar tendency could be observed in Denmark where audiobook sales increased by 58%, see Marie Starup and Jeppe Naur, eds., *Bogen og litteraturens vilkår: Bogpanelets årsrapport 2020* (Slots- og kulturstyrelsen, 2020), https://boghandlerforeningen.dk/wp-content/uploads/2020/11/bogen-og-litteraturens-vilkaar-2020.pdf.
19. See Sara Tanderup Linkis, "Reading Spaces. Original Audiobooks and Mobile Listening," *Soundeffects* 10, no. 1 (2021): 42–55.
20. Ibid.
21. Ibid.

Bibliography

Åberg, Daniel. "At skrive til øret. Betragtninger fra en Storytel Originals forfatter." *Passage* 83 (2020): 71–84.

———. "Daniel Åberg skrev ljudboksserie om dödligt virus men skulle aldrig kalla sig virusexpert." Interview by Sölvé Dahlgren. *Bokugg*, March 16, 2020. www.boktugg.se/2020/03/16/daniel-aberg-skrev-ljudboksserie-om-dodligt-virus-men-skulle-aldrig-kalla-sig-virusexpert/.

———. "Virus författaren avslöjer detaljer vi kan ha missat!" *Storytel's Blog*, April 13, 2017. https://blog.storytel.se/2017/04/13/virus-forfattaren-avslojar-detaljer-vi-kan-ha-missat/.

Allen, Rob, and Thijs van den Berg, eds. *Serialization in Popular Culture*. New York: Routledge, 2014.

Andersen, Carsten. "Dansk forlag vil tage tv-serien tilbage til litteraturens territorium." *Politiken*, October 27, 2016. http://politiken.dk/kultur/boger/art5595116/Dansk-forlag-vil-tage-tv-serien-tilbage-tillitteraturens-territorium.

———. "Nu skal danskerne høre specialdesignede romaner, som vi streamer Netflix-serier." *Politiken*, October 23, 2017. http://politiken.dk/kultur/boger/art6171344/Nu-skal-danskerne-høre-specialdesignederomaner-som-vi-streamer-Netflix-serier.

Andersen, Tore Rye. "Staggered Transmissions: Twitter and the Return of Serialized Literature." *Convergence* 23, no. 1 (2017): 34–48.

———. *Serier*. Aarhus: Aarhus Universitetsforlag, 2019.

Andersen, Tore Rye, and Sara Tanderup Linkis. "As We Speak. Concurrent Narration and Participation in the Serial Narratives *Skam* and '@I_Bombadil'." *Narrative* 27, no. 1 (2019): 83–106.

Anderson, Chris. "The Long Tail." *Wired Magazine*, January 10, 2004. www.wired.com/2004/10/tail/.

Anderson, Porter. "Storytel in Spain: When Entering the Audiobook Market Means Making New Serials." *Publishing Perspectives*, June 6, 2018. https://publishingperspectives.com/2018/06/storytel-spain-audiobook-market-original-serials/.

Atwood, Margaret. "Why Wattpad Works." *The Guardian*, July 6, 2012. www.theguardian.com/books/2012/jul/06/margaret-atwood-wattpad-online-writing.

Atwood, Margaret, and Alderman Naomi. "The Happy Zombie Sunrise Home." *Wattpad*, 2013. www.wattpad.com/8164541-the-happy-zombie-sunrise-home.

Bibliography

Austin, Sara. "Performative Metafiction. Lemony Snicket, Daniel Handler and *the End* of *a Series of Unfortunate Events*." *The Looking Glass: New Perspectives on Children's Literature* 17, no. 1 (2013).

Bangsgaard, Jeppe. "Føljetonen vender tilbage til litteraturen." *Berlingske*, January 5, 2016. www.b.dk/kultur/foeljetonen-vender-tilbage-til-litteraturen.

Berglund, Karl, and Ann Steiner. "Is Backlist the New Frontlist." *Logos* 32, no. 1 (2021): 7–24.

Berglund, Karl, and Sara Tanderup Linkis. "Modelling Subscription-Based Streaming Services for Books." *Memoires du Livre/Studies in Book Culture* (forthcoming).

Björkén Nyberg, Cecilia. "Tolkning, tydlighed och tolkande tydlighet. Tre röstgestaltninger av Hjalmar Söderbergs *Den allvarsamma leken*." In *Från Stringberg till Storytel*, edited by Julia Pennlert and Lars Ilshammar, 137–61. Stockholm: Daidalos, 2021.

Bold, Melanie Ramdarshan. "The Return of the Social Author: Negotiating Authority and Influence on Wattpad." *Convergence* 24, no. 2 (2018): 117–36.

Bolter, Jay David, and Richard Grusin. *Remediation. Understanding New Media*. Cambridge: The MIT Press, 1999.

Bosman, Julie. "Periodic Novel, Coming Soon." *The New York Times*, February 22, 2011. https://mediadecoder.blogs.nytimes.com/2011/11/20/periodic-novel-coming-soon/.

Bullen, Elizabeth. "Power of Darkness: Narrative and Biographical Reflexivity in *a Series of Unfortunate Events*." *International Research in Children's Literature* 1, no. 2 (2008): 200–12.

Butt, Bruce. "'He's Behind You! Reflections on Repetition and Predictability in Lemony Snicket's *a Series of Unfortunate* Events." *Children's Literature in Education* 34, no. 4 (2003): 277–86.

Cantrell, Sarah K. "Nothing Like Pretend. Difference, Disorder and Dystopia in the Multiple World Spaces of Philip Pullman's His Dark Materials." *Children's Literature in Education* 41 (2010): 302–22.

Cecire, Maria Sachiko, Hannah Field, Kavita Mundan Finn, and Malini Roy. "Introduction. Spaces of Power, Places of Play." In *Space and Place in Children's Literature, 1789 to the Present*. New York: Routledge, 2016.

Collins, Jim. *Bring on the Books for Everybody*. Durham and London: Duke UP, 2010.

———. "Fifty Shades of Seriality and E-Readers Games." *Akademisk Kvarter* 7 (2013): 366–79.

———. "The Use Values of Narrativity in Digital Cultures." *New Literary History* 44 (2013): 639–60.

Danielewski, Mark Z. "Building Familiarity." Interview by Javier Calvo, *O Magazine*, 2017. https://abcdefghijklmn-pqrstuvwxyz.com/building-familiarity-interview-with-mark-z-danielewski/.

———. "Clip 4." *Black Clock* 15 (2012): 164–86.

———. "A Conversation with Mark Z. Danielewski." Interview by Philbert Dy, *Rogue Books*, 2017. http://rogue.ph/conversation-mark-z-danielewski/.

———. *The Familiar 1. One Rainy Day in May*. New York: Pantheon, 2014.
———. *The Familiar 2. Into the Forrest*. New York: Pantheon, 2015.
———. *The Familiar 4. Hades*. New York: Pantheon, 2017.
———. *The Familiar 5. Redwood*. New York: Pantheon, 2017.
———. "The Rumpus Interview with Mark Danielewski." Interview by Dylan Foley. *The Rumpus*, May 20, 2015. https://therumpus.net/2015/05/the-rumpus-interview-with-mark-danielewski/.
Davies, Rosamund. "Collaborative Production and the Transformation of Publishing: The Case of Wattpad." In *Collaborative Production in the Creative Industries*, edited by J. Graham and A. Gandini, 51–67. London: University of Westminster Press, 2017.
Eco, Umberto. *The Limits of Interpretation*. Bloomington and Indianapolis: Indiana University Press, 1991.
Eloise, Marianne. "Here's Why a Series of Unfortunate Events' Ending Betray the Best Thing About the Books." *Digital Spy*, January 7, 2019, www.digitalspy.com/tv/a25773647/a-series-of-unfortunate-events-netflix-ending/.
Flood, Alison. "Mark Z Danielewski Wins Seven-Figure Advance for Serial Novel." *The Guardian*, November 22, 2011.
Gibbons, Alison. "Remediation, Storytelling and the Printed Book: The Stylistic Strategies of Mark Z. Danielewski's *the Fifty Year Sword*." In *The Printed Book in Contemporary American Culture*, edited by Heike Schaefer and Alexander Starre, 179–202. Cham: Palgrave Macmillan, 2019.
Goris, An. "Happily Ever After. . . . and After: Serialization and the Popular Romance Novel." *Americana* 12, no. 1 (2013). www.americanpopularculture.com/journal/articles/spring_2013/goris.htm.
Greenwell, Amanda M. "Remodeling Home in Philip Pullman's *His Dark Materials*." *The Lion and the Unicorn* (January 2018): 20–36.
Hagedorn, Roger. "Technology and Economic Exploitation: The Serial as a Form of Narrative Presentation." *Wide Angle* 10, no. 4 (1988): 4–12.
Handler, Daniel. "Fresh Air from WHYY." Interview by Terry Gross, *NPR.org*, December 10, 2001. www.npr.org/templates/story/story.php?storyId=4212818.
Hanner, Hedda, Alice O'Connor, and Erik Wikberg. *Ljudboken. Hur den Digitala Logiken påverkar Marknaden, Konsumptionen och Framtiden*. Stockholm: Svenska Förläggareföreningen, 2019.
Have, Iben, and Mille Raabye Jensen. "Audiobingeing. Storytel Originals som produkt af en streaming kultur." *Passage* 83 (2020): 67–84.
Have, Iben, and Birgitte Stougaard Pedersen. "The Audiobook Circuit in Digital Publishing: Voicing the Silent Revolution." *New Media & Society* 22, no. 3 (2020): 409–28.
———. *Digital Audiobooks: New Media, Users and Experiences*. New York: Routledge, 2016.
Hayles, N. Katherine. *Writing Machines*. Cambridge, MA: MIT Press, 2002.
Hayward, Jennifer Poole. *Consuming Pleasures: Active Audiences and Serial Fictions from Dickens to Soap Opera*. Lexington: University Press of Kentucky, 1997.

Hunt, Peter. "Landscapes and Journeys, Metaphors and Maps: The Distinctive Feature of English Fantasy." *Children's Literature Association Quarterly* 12, no. 1 (1987): 11–14.

Hutcheon, Linda. "Harry Potter and the Novice's Confession." *The Lion and the Unicorn* 32, no. 2 (2008): 169–79.

———. *A Theory of Adaptation*. New York: Routledge, 2006.

"Hvad er Mofibo Originals." *Mofibo Support*, June 22, 2021. https://support.mofibo.com/hc/da/articles/115001070410-Hvad-er-en-Mofibo-Original.

Jeffery, Morgan. "Neil Patrick Harris Reveals Why a Series of Unfortunate Events Is Ending After Season 3." *Digital Spy*, March 29, 2018. www.digitalspy.com/tv/ustv/news/a853528/a-series-of-unfortunate-events-season-2-neil-patrick-harris-interview/.

Jenkins, Henry. *Convergence Culture. Where Old and New Media Collide*. New York and London: New York University Press, 2006.

———. "The Cultural Logic of Media Convergence." *International Journal of Cultural Studies* 7, no. 1 (2004): 33–43.

———. "Transmedial Storytelling 101." *Confessions of an Aca-Fan*, March 21, 2007. http://henryjenkins.org/blog/2007/03/transmedia_storytelling_101.html.

Johnson, Miriam. "The Rise of the Citizen Author. Writing Within Social Media." *Publishing Research Quarterly* 33, no. 2 (2017): 131–46.

Kaczyńska, Barbara. "Metafiction in Children's Literature and Its Adaptation on Screen. The Case of Lemony Snicket's a Series of Unfortunate Events." *New Horizons in English Studies* 3 (2018): 71–85.

Kashka, Boris. "Audiobooks Are the New Ebooks. Except They Might Keep Growing." *Vulture*, September 20, 2018. www.vulture.com/2018/09/audiobooks-are-booming-but-how-long-will-that-last.html.

Kelleter, Frank. "Five Ways of Looking at Popular Seriality." In *Media of Serial Narrative*, edited by Frank Kelleter, 7–37. Columbus: The Ohio State University Press, 2017.

———. "From Recursive Progression to Systemic Self-Observation. Elements of a Theory of Seriality." *Velvet Light Trap* 79 (2017): 99–105.

———, ed. *Media of Serial Narrative*. Columbus: The Ohio State University Press, 2017.

———. "Populäre Serialität: Eine Einführung." In *Populäre Serialität*, edited by Frank Kelleter, 11–46. Bielefeld: transcript Verlag, 2014.

———. *Serial Agencies. The Wire and Its Readers*. Hants: Zero Books, 2013.

Kermode, Frank. *The Sense of an Ending*. Oxford: Oxford University Press, 1967.

Kirscher, Madison Malone. "This Woman Wrote Fan-Fic on Her Phone and Ended Up with a Major Book Deal." *Business Insider*, July 28, 2015. www.businessinsider.com/anna-todd-earns-book-and-movie-deals-for-one-direction-fan-fiction-2015-7?r=UK&IR=T.

Latham, Sean, and Scholes, Robert. "The Rise of Periodical Studies." *PMLA* 121, no. 2 (2006): 517–31.

Loughrey, Clarisse. "A Series of Unfortunate Events Season 2 Review: Misery Makes a Welcome Return." *Independent*, March 30, 2018. www.independent.co.uk/arts-entertainment/tv/reviews/a-series-of-unfortunate-events-season-2-review-release-watch-netflix-date-cast-count-olaf-a8274776.html.

Magnussen, Kendra. "Lemony Snicket's *a Series of Unfortunate Events*: Daniel Handler and Marketing the Author." *Children's Literature Association Quarterly* 37, no. 1 (2012): 86–107.

McGann, Jerome, *The Textual Condition*. Princeton: Princeton University Press, 1991.

Miller, Monica. "What Wattpad Brings to the Publishing Table." *PUB 800*, December 9, 2015. https://tkbr.publishing.sfu.ca/pub800/2015/12/what-wattpad-brings-to-the-table/.

Miller, Peggy J., and Jaqueline J. Goodnow. "Cultural Practices: Toward an Integration of Culture and Development." *New Directions for Child Development* 67 (1995): 5–16.

Mittell, Jason. *Complex TV. The Poetics of Contemporary Television Storytelling*. New York: New York University Press, 2015.

———. "Sites of Participation. Wiki Fandom and the Case of Lostpedia." *Transformative Works and Cultures* 3 (2009). https://doi.org/10.3983/twc.2009.0118.

Moore, Anne. "After the Break. Serial Narratives and Fannish Reading." Diss., Tufts University, 2012.

Murray, Padmini Ray, and Claire Squires. "The Digital Publishing Communications Circuit." *Book 2.0* 3, no. 1 (2013): 3–24.

Nielsen, Jakob Isak. "Tv-serien som vòr tids roman?" *Passage* 68 (2012): 83–100.

Nodelman, Perry. *The Hidden Adult: Defining Children's Literature*. Baltimore: Johns Hopkins University Press, 2008.

Nolin, Jan, and Elisa Wallin. "Time to Read: Exploring the Time Spaces of Subscription-Based Audiobooks." *New Media & Society* 22, no. 3 (2020): 1–19.

Oltean, Tudor. "Series and Seriality in Media Culture." *European Journal of Communication* 8 (1993): 5–31.

"Originals." *Storytel Publishing*, 2021. https://publishing.storytel.com/sg/originals/.

Page, Ruth. "Seriality and Storytelling in Social Media." *Storyworlds: A Journal of Narrative Studies* 5 (2013): 31–54.

Patten, Robert L. "Dickens as Serial Author. A Case of Multiple Identities." In *Nineteenth Century Media and the Construction of Identities*, edited by Laurel Brake, Bill Bell and David Finkelstein, 137–53. London: Palgrave Macmillan, 2000.

Pressman, Jessica. "The Aesthetics of Bookishness in Twenty-First-Century Literature." *Bookishness: The New Fate of Reading in the Digital Age. Michigan Quarterly Review* 48 (2009). http://hdl.handle.net/2027/spo.act2080.0048.402.

———. *Bookishness. Loving Books in the Digital Age*. New York: Columbia University Press, 2020.

Pullman, Philip. *His Dark Materials*. London: Scholastic, 2012.

———. "Let's Write It in Red: The Patrick Hardy Lecture." *Signal* 85 (1998): 44–62.

———. *Lyra's Oxford*. New York: Doubleday, Penguin Random House, 2017.

———. "Questions and Answers." *Philip Pullman* (website), 2009. www.philip-pullman.com/qas?searchtext=&page=5.

———. *The Secret Commonwealth*. London: Penguin Books LTD, 2019.

Rizzo, Lillian, and Drew Fitzgerald. "Forget the Streaming Wars—Pandemic-Stricken 2020 Lifted Netflix and Others." *The Wall Street Journal*, December 30, 2020. www.wsj.com/articles/forget-the-streaming-warspandemic-stricken-2020-lifted-netflix-and-others-11609338780.

Rubery, Matthew. "Play It Again, Sam Weller. New Digital Audiobooks and Old Ways of Reading." *Journal of Victorian Culture* 13, no. 1 (2010): 58–79.

———. *The Untold Story of the Talking Book*. Cambridge, MA: Harvard University Press, 2016.

Ryan, Marie-Laure. "Space." In *The Living Handbook of Narratology*, edited by Peter Hühn. Hamburg: Hamburg University, 2012. www.lhn.uni-hamburg.de/node/55.html.

———. "Story/World/Media. Turning the Instruments of a Media-Conscious Narratology." In *Storyworlds Across Media. Toward a Media-Conscious Narratology*, edited by Marie-Laure Ryan and Jan-Noël Thon, 25–49. Lincoln and London: University of Nebraska Press, 2014.

Ryan, Marie-Laure, and Jan-Noël Thon, eds. *Storyworlds Across Media. Toward a Media-Conscious Narratology*. Lincoln and London: University of Nebraska Press, 2014.

Ryan, Marie-Laure, Kenneth Foote, and Maoz Azaryahu. *Narrating Space/Spatializing Narrative. Where Narrative Theory and Geography Meet*. Columbus: The Ohio State University Press, 2016.

A Series of Unfortunate Events: The Complete Wreck. Harper Collins, October 13, 2006. www.harpercollins.ca/9780061119064/a-series-of-unfortunate-events-box-the-complete-wreck-books-1–13/.

A Series of Unfortunate Events, season 1, episode 2, "The Bad Beginning—Part Two." Developed by Mark Hudis and Barry Sonnenfeld. Netflix, 2017.

A Series of Unfortunate Events, season 1, episode 3, "The Reptile Room—Part One." Developed by Mark Hudis and Barry Sonnenfeld. Netflix, 2017.

A Series of Unfortunate Events, season 1, episode 7, "The Miserable Mill—Part One." Developed by Mark Hudis and Barry Sonnenfeld. Netflix, 2017.

A Series of Unfortunate Events, season 1, episode 8, "The Miserable Mill—Part Two." Developed by Mark Hudis and Barry Sonnenfeld. Netflix, 2017.

A Series of Unfortunate Events, season 2, episode 10, "The Carnivorous Carnival—Part Two." Developed by Mark Hudis and Barry Sonnenfeld. Netflix, 2018.

A Series of Unfortunate Events, season 3, episode 7, "The End." Developed by Mark Hudis and Barry Sonnenfeld. Netflix, 2019.

Schwindt, Oriana. "'A Series of Unfortunate Events' Renewed for Season Two at Netflix." *Variety*, March 13, 2017. https://variety.com/2017/tv/news/a-series-of-unfortunate-events-renewed-season-2-netflix-1202007658/.

Sielke, Sabine. "'Joy in Repetition': The Significance of Seriality for Memory and (Re)Mediation." In *The Memory Effect: The Remediation of Memory in Literature and Film*, edited by Russell Kilbourn and Eleanor Ty, 37–50. Waterloo: Wilfrid Laurier University Press, 2013.

Snicket, Lemony. *The Bad Beginning*. New York: HarperCollins, 1999.

———. *The End*. New York: HarperCollins, 2006.

———. *The Reptile Room*. New York: HarperCollins, 1999.

———. *The Wide Window*. New York: HarperCollins, 2000.

Squires, Claire. *Marketing Literature*. London: Palgrave Macmillan, 2009.

Starup, Marie, and Jeppe Naur, eds. *Bogen og litteraturens vilkår: Bogpanelets årsrapport 2020*. Copenhagen: Slots- og kulturstyrelsen, 2020. https://boghandlerforeningen.dk/wp-content/uploads/2020/11/bogen-og-litteraturens-vilkaar-2020.pdf.

Steiner, Ann. "Serendipity, Promotion, and Literature." In *Hype. Bestsellers and Literary Culture*, edited by Jon Helgason, Sara Kärrholm and Ann Steiner, 41–56. Lund: Nordic Academic Press, 2014.

Storytel. *Annual Report and Sustainability Report*. Stockholm: Storytel, 2020. https://investors.storytel.com/en/wp-content/uploads/sites/2/2021/04/storytel-annual-report-2020-storytel-ab-publ-210401.pdf.

Stougaard Pedersen, Birgitte. "At skrive gennem lyd." *Passage* 83 (2020): 85–99.

Tanderup Linkis, Sara. "'The Form Itself Begins to Vanish': Seriality and Multimodality in Mark Z. Danielewski's *the Familiar*." In *Fictionality and Multimodal Narratives*, edited by Alison Gibbons and Torsa Ghosal. Lincoln and London: University of Nebraska Press, forthcoming.

———. "'It's Off-Book!' Developing Serial Complexity Across Media in *A Series of Unfortunate Events*." *Children's Literature Association Quarterly* 45, no. 1 (2020): 59–79.

———. "Läsning i rörelse. Platsens betydelse i Storytels ljudfodda berättelser." In *Från Stringberg till Storytel*, edited by Julia Pennlert and Lars Ilshammar, 269–94. Stockholm: Daidalos, 2021.

———. "Literary Remediations of Contemporary Television Series." In *Television Series as Literature*, edited by Reto Winckler and Victor Huertas-Martín. Shanghai: Palgrave Macmillan, 2021.

———. "Reading Spaces. Original Audiobooks and Mobile Listening." *Soundeffects* 10, no. 1 (2021): 42–55.

———. "Resonant Listening. Local Voices and Places in Born-Audio Literary Narratives." In *Resonance and the Echo Chamber of Reading*, edited by Shuangyi Li. *Canadian Review of Comparative Literature/Revue canadienne de littérature compare* 47, no. 4 (2021): 404–23.

———. "Volumes! Den litterære serie mellem medier." *Passage* 79 (2018): 117–34.

Tanderup Linkis, Sara, and Julia Pennlert. "Episodic Listening: Analysing the Usage and Content of Born-Audio Serials." *Journal of Electronic Publishing* 20, no. 3, 2021. https://doi.org/10.3998/3336451.0023.102.

———. "It Adds a Dimension." Paper presented at the conference "Revolutions in Reading," Stockholm University, Stockholm, June 22, 2021.

Thomas, Bronwen. "Trickster Authors and Tricky Readers on the MZD forums." In *Mark Z. Danielewski*, edited by Joe Bray and Alison Gibbons, 86–102. Manchester: Manchester University Press, 2011.

———. "Update Soon! Harry Potter Fanfiction and Narrative as a Participatory Process." In *New Narratives: Stories and Storytelling in the Digital Age*, edited by Ruth Page and Bronwen Thomas, 205–19. Lincoln: University of Nebraska Press, 2011.

Thompson, John B. *Book Wars. The Digital Revolution in Publishing*. Cambridge: Polity Press, 2021.

———. *Merchants of Culture*. London: Penguin, 2012.

Tuan, Yi-Fu. *Space and Place: The Perspective of Experience*. Minneapolis: University of Minnesota Press, 1977.
Turner, Mark W. "The Unruliness of Serials in the Nineteenth Century (and in the Digital Age)." In *Serialization in Popular Culture*, edited by Rob Allen and Theis van den Berg, 11–31. New York: Routledge, 2014.
Vadde, Aarthi. "Amateur Creativity. Contemporary Literature and the Digital Publishing Scene." *New Literary History* 48 (2017): 27–51.
van de Ven, Inge. "The Serial Novel in an Age of Binging. How to Read Mark Z. Danielewski's the Familiar." *Image & Narrative* 17, no. 4 (2016): 92–103.
Wattpad FAQ, 2019. www.wattpad.com/writers/faq/.
Wattpad writers' forum, 2019. "Should I post my whole novel all at once or serialize it": www.wattpadwriters.com/t/should-i-post-my-whole-novel-all-at-once-or-serialize-it/99503.h.
Wikberg, Erik. *Bokförsäljningsstatistiken: Helåret 2020*. Stockholm: Svenska Förläggareföreningen, 2021.
Winckler, Reto, and Victor Huertas-Martín, eds. *Television Series as Literature*. Shanghai: Palgrave Macmillan, 2021.

Index

Åberg, Daniel 11, 13n13, 70, 77–82, 108
adaptation 6, 105–6; of *A Series of Unfortunate Events* 34–5, 37, 41–8, 50n26; of *His Dark Materials* 53, 62–6
advertisements 27, 90, 98
affordances 9, 29, 106; of audiobooks 69, 71, 75–6; of the printed book 16, 22; of streaming television 41; *see also* medium specificity
After 11, 87, 89, 93–8, 105; *see also* Todd, Anna
Alderman, Naomi 11, 86, 91–2, 98, 101n24
amateur writing 86–9, 91–5
Amber Spyglass, The see His Dark Materials
Atwood, Margaret 5, 6, 11, 86–7, 91–2, 98–9
Audible 71
audiences 3, 6, 46; active 9, 106–7; adult 65–6; building 9, 69–70, 74–6, 93; niche 24; serial 27, 79, 88; *see also* participatory culture; reading communities
audiobook boom 71
audiobooks 1, 5, 69–82, 109; consumption of 11, 71–4, 81–2; digital 5, 70–71, 106
author 33n45, 86–100; amateur 87–8, 93–7; communication 25–6; fictional 40, 43; professional 90–2; serial 75, 78, 84n23; *see also* citizen author; collective production

backlist 74, 108
Beatrice Letters, The 37, 47–8; *see also* Snicket, Lemony
bestsellers 5–6, 108
bildungsroman 52, 54
bingeing 5, 43, 76
book-blogging 89
book history 3, 4, 7
bookishness 10, 21–4, 34, 106
book market 5, 81; digital 69–70
Book of Dust, The 52, 58–62, 66
born-audio literature 69–82; *see also* audiobooks; Storytel

capitalism 37, 107
children's literature 10, 34–6, 46, 48, 52–4, 65; Victorian 40
citizen author 88, 91
closure 39, 42, 47–8, 54; *see also* endings
co-creation 27; *see also* collective production; participatory culture
collaboration 26, 86, 91–2, 99, 107
collaborative creation 17, 107; *see also* collective production
collective production 17, 26, 31n9, 75
continuation, serial 28, 37, 51n46, 77, 79, 95
convergence culture 30, 75, 87, 106; *see also* media convergence
copyright 75
Covid19 81, 108

Danielewski, Mark Z. 1, 10, 15–33, 88, 103–4; *see also The Familiar*; *House of Leaves*; *Only Revolutions*

Index

democratization 9, 86–9, 91–2, 98–9, 107; of print 2; *see also* collaboration; participatory culture
Dickens, Charles 2–3, 9, 21, 25, 30, 110; and oral performance 73, 82; and reader culture 86, 88, 91, 107
digital culture 9, 72, 82, 86–7, 98–9
digitalization 2, 4–5, 9, 11, 99; of audiobooks 69–71; and printed books 22; and social media 88–9, 107; *see also* digital culture
duration, serial 21–4, 29, 104

Eco, Umberto 8, 20, 24, 35–7, 93, 104–5, 109–10
Egan, Jennifer 5, 13n13
endings 8, 39, 45–8, 58, 88, 103; happy 35–6, 93; *see also* closure
episodic format 16, 41–2, 76, 82, 103–5

Facebook 15, 20, 22, 24–9, 82, 88; *see also* social media
Familiar, The 1, 9–10, 15–33, 34–5, 48, 69, 88, 103–4
familiarity 18–20, 24, 36, 57, 66, 109–10
fan culture 9, 25–7, 48, 93–9; *see also* collaborative creation; fanfiction; participatory culture
fanfiction 51n46, 87, 89, 93–9
fantasy fiction 54, 62
feedback 8, 27, 106; on Storytel 78; on Wattpad 86–7, 90–1, 94–8
Ferrante, Elena 5, 24
feuilleton novels 1, 3, 8, 21, 30, 72–3, 94, 105; *see also* Victorian culture

Golden Compass, The see His Dark Materials
Gothic fiction 36
generations 86, 91–2

Hagedorn, Roger 3–5, 70, 73–4, 103–4
Handler, Daniel 10, 34, 37–8, 40, 43; *see also* Snicket, Lemony
Handmaid's Tale, The 6
Happy Zombie Sunrise Home, The 11, 86–7, 91–2

Harry Potter 9, 24, 34
His Dark Materials 5, 10–11, 52–67, 104; film adaptation 63; original trilogy 55–58; storyworld 53, 5, 59, 62–3; television adaptation 62–6, 106
House of Leaves 17, 25, 30n2

intertextuality 35–6

Jenkins, Henry: on convergence culture 30, 106–7; on participatory culture 9, 25, 27, 87–9, 91, 99; on transmedia storytelling 6, 35, 42, 46–7, 105; *see also* convergence culture; participatory culture; transmedia storytelling

Kelleter, Frank 4–5, 7, 25, 27–8, 79, 88; on capitalism 37, 107
Knausgaard, Karl Ove 5, 15, 24

La Belle Sauvage see The Book of Dust
literary sociology 7, 9
long tail logic 80
Lyra's Oxford 52, 57, 59–60, 66

mass media 3–5, 7
maturation 52–62, 65–7, 104
media convergence 6, 9, 25, 70; *see also* convergence culture
medium specificity 9, 10, 29, 70, 76, 81–2, 105–6
meta-reflexivity 36, 39, 42
micro-celebrities 96
Mittell, Jason 8–9, 16, 20–1, 27, 42–5, 104–5
mobility 94, 99
multimodality 23, 104
multiple worlds 52, 56–8, 64
multitasking 72, 75

narrative complexity 8, 66, 104–5; in *A Series of Unfortunate Events* 35–48; in *The Familiar* 16, 20–21
Netflix 29, 34, 41–3, 46–7, 108; Originals 69

Only Revolutions 25, 31n17

parody 36, 55
participatory culture 9, 25, 78–9, 86–9, 106–7; and *The Familiar* 25–8; and storyworlds 60; on Wattpad 89–96, 98–9
pandemic 79, 81, 108–10
platforms 5–6, 11, 30, 55, 93, 110; consumption on 70, 74, 81–2; *see also* Storytel; Wattpad
penny dreadfuls 30
podcasts 76, 81–2, 83n11, 85n48
popular culture 2, 3–5, 7, 20, 87, 106
popularization, of literature 3–4, 106
postmodernism 36
predictability 24, 105, 110
prequels 17, 24, 52, 59
prosumers 27, 87, 107, 110
publishing 75–6; digital 88–9, 99–100, 103, 111; industry 70, 72, 82; self- 89, 98; serial 7, 9, 11, 17, 21, 37, 80, 86, 90–1, 98; social media 22; traditional 93
publishing studies 4, 9
Pullman, Philip 5, 8, 10–11, 52–68, 103, 105–6, 108; *see also The Book of Dust*; *His Dark Materials*; *Lyra's Oxford*

reader communities 9, 11, 25–8, 32n38, 86–102, 107; *see also* readers; reading
reader 3; active 15, 24–8, 78–9, 86–92, 107; audiobook 71–5; child 38–40, 48; expectations 36–7; experience 20, 53–5, 57, 62, 64–7, 71; loyalty 74, 90–1, 108; turned-viewers 46; *see also* reader communities; reading
reading 11, 24, 41, 76; and maturation 46; as salvation 39, 92; serial 57; social 9, 25–8, 73, 86–92, 99; and rereading 23, 78, 97; *see also* reader
remediation 11, 15–16, 21, 28, 30, 71, 105
repetition, serial 8, 20, 104–5, 110; in *After* 93; in *A Series of Unfortunate Events* 34–8, 41–2; in *His Dark Materials* 65–6
romance 72, 93

Secret Commonwealth, The see *The Book of Dust*

self-referentiality 43–4
seriality: bookish 15–16, 22, 24, 29–30, 106; and capitalism 37–8; definition of 2, 8; and mass media 3–4; and popular culture 7, 73, 87; *see also* serialization
serialization: as a business model 6, 69–70, 73, 90, 107–8; as a cultural practice 11–12, 110; definition of 2–3; digital 5, 13n13, 90, 99–100, 107; history of 2–7; resurgence of 1, 5; and social aspects 9, 87–8; as a transmedial practice 2, 6, 10, 28, 30, 52, 105
Series of Unfortunate Events, A 5, 10, 34–48, 64, 108; *see also* Snicket, Lemony
shelveability 21–2, 34, 49n2
sign iconic representation 19, 31n15
Snicket, Lemony 5, 8, 10, 34–48, 65, 103–6, 108; *see also A Series of Unfortunate Events*; Handler, Daniel
soap opera 88, 95
social media 5, 22, 88–9, 92, 98, 106–7; reading cultures on 25–8, 32n38, 32n40; *see also* Facebook; Wattpad
space 52–5; democratic 88, 91, 98; in *His Dark Materials* 55–9, 66–7, 104; and place 10–11
spaciousness 52–3, 54, 58, 67
spatial turn 55
spin-offs 37, 47, 79–80
Storytel 1, 5–6, 11, 69–85, 98–9, 103, 105–11; *see also* audiobooks
storyworlds 8, 10, 53–5, 60, 103, 107
Stranger Things 15, 25
streaming 6, 81–2, 108–9, 110, 112 n17; audiobooks 69–74; television 41, 44
Subtle Knife, The see *His Dark Materials*

television 3, 7, 98; audience 9, 41, 107; *see also* television series
television series 3, 8–9, 17, 63–4, 69, 73–7, 81–2, 103–6; complex 8, 21–2, 35, 42–5; and literature 1, 10–11, 15–16, 28–9, 41, 48, 106; production 17, 26, 43; quality 6
temporality: serial 44, 54, 77

Todd, Anna 11, 87, 89, 93–8, 105, 108
transmedia complexity 8, 10, 45–7, 105–6
transmediality 6–7, 15, 28–9, 87, 105–6, 108
transmedia storytelling 6, 9, 34–5, 42–3, 46, 110
typographic experiments 1, 18–20, 23

unruliness 105, 108
updating 90, 94–5, 98

Victorian culture: book design 34; and feuilleton novels 2–3, 7, 91, 105; and performative reading 73; and social norms 56
Virus 11, 70, 77–82, 100, 108

waiting 25, 94
Wattpad 2, 11, 78, 86–102, 103, 107–8
worldbuilding 105–6, 110

For Product Safety Concerns and Information please contact our EU
representative GPSR@taylorandfrancis.com
Taylor & Francis Verlag GmbH, Kaufingerstraße 24, 80331 München, Germany

www.ingramcontent.com/pod-product-compliance
Lightning Source LLC
Chambersburg PA
CBHW070739230426
43669CB00014B/2505